HENRY VIII

I HENRY VIII
Detail of a portrait by Hans Holbein

HENRY VIII

and his Times

J. J. BAGLEY

ARCO PUBLISHING COMPANY, Inc.
NEW YORK

First published 1963 *in the United States by*
ARCO PUBLISHING COMPANY, Inc.
480 Lexington Avenue, New York 17, N.Y.

© *J. J. Bagley, 1962*

Library of Congress Catalog Card Number: 63-17098
ARCO Catalog Number: 1092

Printed in Great Britain

PREFACE

IN the whole of English history there is hardly a more controversial character than Henry VIII. Certainly no other person has been more discussed. Since his death his private life and his public policy have inspired both praise and condemnation. He ruled England, Wales, and Ireland for the best part of 40 years, but his reign is remarkable and important not for its length but for its achievements. So much of medieval England died, and so much of modern England was born between 1509 and 1547.

All who write on any aspect of the reign of Henry VIII can enjoy a large quarry of primary material in the 21 volumes of *Letters and Papers, Foreign and Domestic, of the Reign of Henry VIII*. Almost all my quotations in modern spelling are taken from this monumental collection made by three scholars, J. S. Brewer, J. Gairdner, and R. H. Brodie, between 1862 and 1920. The unacknowledged quotations in archaic spelling are mostly taken from the 1904 edition of Edward Hall's *The Triumphant Reigne of King Henry VIII*. It has not been considered appropriate in a biography of this length to give detailed references, but it would be less than barest justice not to acknowledge my debt to the following studies made by other historians:

Byrne, M. St. Clare, *The Letters of King Henry VIII*, 1936.
Chambers, R. W., *Thomas More*, 1935.
Doernberg, E., *Henry VIII and Luther*, 1961.
Elton, G. R., *The Tudor Revolution in Government*, 1959.
Ferguson, C., *Naked to Mine Enemies*, 1958.
Friedmann, P., *Anne Boleyn*, 1884.
Hackett, F., *Henry the Eighth*, 1929.
Knowles, D., *The Religious Orders in England*, Vol. III, 1959.
Mattingly, G., *Catherine of Aragon*, 1942.
Mackie, J. D., *The Earlier Tudors, 1485–1558*, 1952.
MacNalty, A. S., *Henry VIII: a difficult patient*, 1952.
Pollard, A. F., *Henry VIII*, 1902.
   Wolsey, 1929.
Prescott, H. F. M., *Spanish Tudor*, 1940.

7

Savage, H. (ed.), *The Love Letters of Henry VIII*, 1949.

Smith, L. B., *A Tudor Tragedy*, 1961.

Smith, H. M., *Henry VIII and the Reformation*, 1948.

Sturge, C., *Cuthbert Tunstal*, 1938.

Tanner, J. R., *Tudor Constitutional Documents, 1485–1603*, 1922.

Zeeveld, W. G., *Foundations of Tudor Policy*, 1948

Once again I am particularly indebted for the ready help of my wife and of my two colleagues and friends, Dr. A. R. Myers and Miss Joan Beck.

J.J.B.

University of Liverpool
Spring, 1962.

CONTENTS

Preface   7

Acknowledgment   10

List of Illustrations   11

1 PROMISE AND IMMATURITY   13
   *Henry's Inheritance—The Marriage of Henry and
   Catherine—The New Régime—Henry's Diplomatic
   Apprenticeship—Wolsey's Early Career—Henry and
   Francis.*

2 HENRY AND WOLSEY   34
   *Henry Seeks an Ally—Buckingham and Luther Con-
   demned—Renewed War Against France*

3 THE INADEQUACY OF WOLSEY   57
   *The Boleyn Family—Henry Broaches His Great Matter
   —Campeggio in England—Changes in Council*

4 SEPARATION FROM ROME   81
   *Anne's Triumph—The Coronation of Queen Anne—
   Other People's Consciences—The Act of Succession*

5 THE BLOCK AND THE GALLOWS   107
   *The End of Anne Boleyn—The Northern Rising—The
   Birth of Edward VI—Threat of Invasion*

6 ACTIVITY IN SPITE OF INFIRMITY   128
   *Anne of Cleves—A Second Queen Catherine—War
   Against Scotland—War Against France—The Father
   of His People*

Index   152

ACKNOWLEDGMENT

Figures 7, 10, 12, 14, 15, 16, 20, 24 are reproduced by gracious permission of Her Majesty The Queen.

The Author and Publishers also wish to thank the following for permission to reproduce the illustrations appearing in this book:

Society of Antiquaries of London, for fig. 5.

The Ashmolean Museum, for fig. 19.

The Earl of Bradford, for fig. 9.

The Trustees of the British Museum, for figs. 25, 26, 27.

The Church Commissioners, for fig. 13.

George Howard, Esq., for fig. 18.

The Keeper of the Kunstmuseum, Basle, for fig. 21.

Kunsthistorisches Museum, Vienna, for fig. 8.

National Maritime Museum, for fig. 4.

The National Portrait Gallery, for figs. 6, 17, 22, 23, 28.

The President and Fellows of St. John's College, Oxford, for fig. 11.

Baron H. H. Thyssen-Bornemisza, for fig. 1.

The Wallace Collection, for figs. 2, 3.

LIST OF ILLUSTRATIONS

Figure

1 Henry VIII
   Detail of a portrait by Hans Holbein   *Frontispiece*

Facing page

2 Charles V of Spain
   Detail of a contemporary Flemish portrait   16

3 Francis I of France
   Detail of a contemporary portrait   16

4 Greenwich Palace
   Detail of an early seventeenth-century painting   17

5 Richmond Palace
   Engraved by James Basire   17

6 Cardinal Wolsey
   Detail of a contemporary portrait by an unknown artist   30

7 Archbishop Warham
   Detail of the drawing by Hans Holbein   30

8 Catherine of Aragon
   Detail of a portrait by Meister Michael   31

9 Anne Boleyn
   Detail of the drawing by Hans Holbein   31

10 Jane Seymour
   Detail of the drawing by Hans Holbein   31

11 Anne of Cleves
   Detail of a contemporary German portrait   31

12 Catherine Howard
   Detail of a contemporary miniature   31

13 Catherine Parr
   Detail of an anonymous portrait   31

14 The Departure of Henry from Dover for the Field of the Cloth of Gold
   Detail from the contemporary painting at Hampton Court   46

15 Henry at the Field of the Cloth of Gold
   Detail from the contemporary painting at Hampton Court   47

16 Sir Thomas More
   Detail of the drawing by Hans Holbein   86

Figure   *Facing page*

17 John Fisher
      From a contemporary copy of a portrait by Hans Holbein   86

18 Henry VIII
      From the portrait by Hans Holbein, 1542   87

19 The Princess Mary
      Detail of an anonymous portrait   102

20 The Princess Elizabeth
      Detail of an anonymous portrait   102

21 Edward, Prince of Wales
      From a chalk and watercolour drawing by Hans Holbein   103

22 Thomas Cromwell, Earl of Essex
      Detail of a portrait after Hans Holbein   110

23 Thomas Cranmer
      Detail of a portrait by G. Flicke   110

24 Henry VIII and Prince Edward
      From a contemporary cameo   111

25 Henry VIII
      From a lead medal by Hans Schwartz   111

26 Henry with his jester
      From a psalter by John Mallard   134

27 Henry reading
      From a psalter by John Mallard   134

28 'The Protestant Succession'. Henry on his deathbed,
      with Edward VI and the Council
      From an anonymous painting   135

LINE ILLUSTRATIONS IN THE TEXT

                                                            Page
Title-page of Henry's attack on Luther, 1521   56

Henry's signature   80

Henry in State   106
  From a Wolsey patent, 1530

The *Henry Grâce-à-Dieu*, 1512   127

Henry VIII in Council   132
  Woodcut by Jacob Faber in Edward Hall's Chronicle

1 PROMISE AND IMMATURITY

'... the indubitate flower, and very heire of both the sayd lineages.'
EDWARD HALL

The morowe folowyng beyng sondaie, and also Midsomer daie [1509], this noble prince with his Quene, at time convenient, under their Canabies borne by the Barons of the five Portes, went from the saied Palaice [Westminster Palace], to Westminster Abbey upon clothe, called vulgarly cloth of Ray, the whiche clothe was cut and spoyled, by the rude and common people, immediatly after their repaire into the Abbey, where, accordyng to the sacred observaunce, and auncient custome his grace with the Quene, were annoynted and crouned, by the Archebusshop of Cantorbury. . . .

THE central figure in all this coronation pageantry, which the contemporary historian, Edward Hall, described in great detail, was Henry Tudor, not quite 18 years old, but already outstanding in physical prowess, and full of promise as a scholar. His tall, well-nourished, youthful figure seemed to ensure a long vigorous reign. His own generation approved his eagerness for hunting, riding, and jousting, and even those whose years had diminished their enthusiasm for robust sports could not help but admire Henry's interest and achievement in classical learning and music. Ability in a prince is apt to prompt extravagant praise, but with this young king courtiers had no need to dissemble '"How clever" at whatsoever he condescended to say'. His skill on horseback and in feats of strength was self-evident; his Latin scholarship won high praise from Erasmus, who could censure as well as flatter princes, and both his dexterity in playing the lute, the organ, and the virginals and his delight in listening to his minstrels at court and his choristers in the chapel royal could not help but awaken excited interest and comment. He even composed music, and the most long-lived of his many pieces, the anthem, 'O Lord, the Maker of all things', and the song, 'Pastime with good Company', are occasionally sung today.

Naturally, the accession of this young Apollo roused high hopes. 'Everyone here', Lord Mountjoy informed Erasmus in his extravagant way, 'is rejoicing in the possession of so great a Prince. . . . The heavens laugh, the earth exults, all things are full of milk, of honey, of nectar'.

Henry VIII's Descent from both Lancaster and York

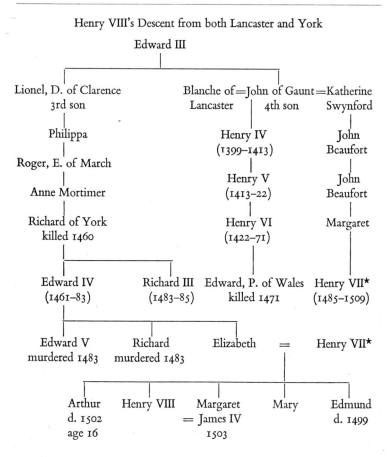

Henry VII's father, Edmund, was the son of Owen Tudor and Catherine of France, the widow of Henry V. Such descent, however, gave him no claim at all to the English throne. Through his mother, Margaret Beaufort, he was descended from Edward III, but if he was going to claim through a woman, he could hardly deny the prior claim of the Yorkists. For this reason he exalted the 'divine right' granted by his victory at Bosworth, and confirmed later by Act of Parliament. He married Elizabeth of York as an extra precaution against the claims of pretenders.

Many of those who crowded Westminster Abbey for the coronation of Henry VIII and his queen had witnessed the accession of his father, and almost as many remembered the strife and confusion which had followed the death of his grandfather, Edward IV. Happily, this latest occasion seemed to be significantly different. No potential rival was challenging the young king's right to succeed to the throne; above all, Henry looked capable of providing for many years to come that firm, positive rule which most people wanted. To banish the nightmare of the Lancaster-York dynastic struggle from their minds, Englishmen were eager to believe without question that their 'Octavius' combined the claims of both contesting houses, and so made impossible any further attack of the wasting disease of civil strife upon England's body politic. Even so, the thoughtful among them realised by how narrow a margin this most desirable and hopeful situation existed.

Henry's Inheritance

Henry VIII was the only surviving son of Henry VII, the self-appointed champion of the Lancastrian cause, and of Elizabeth, the eldest daughter of the Yorkist Edward IV. His thin, consumptive, elder brother, Arthur, had died in 1502 at the age of 16; his younger brother, Edmund, born in 1499, had failed to last a year. True he had two healthy sisters, Margaret and Mary, one of whom would have been proclaimed queen had he, like his brothers, died within his father's lifetime. But England did not want a queen to succeed to the throne. A queen would have a consort—Elizabeth I had not yet demonstrated her short-term solution to this perennial problem—and since it was deemed neither fitting nor politically wise for a queen to marry one of her own subjects, her marriage would inevitably tie England to a foreign alliance and probably to another country's foreign policy. Henry's vigorous survival would spare England from that humiliation. For the last six years Margaret had been the queen of James IV of Scotland, but unmarried Mary could still be used to seal a European alliance. As queens of foreign countries they would expect to be abandoned by the country of their birth if changing political needs required it.

In 1509 England was beginning to enjoy its strength as a nation state. For much of the second half of the previous century, it had housed two struggling factions, whose strife had been unduly prolonged by periodic foreign help. The steadily unifying France of Louis XI and the disruptive, reactionary power of the French princes led by the duke of Burgundy had each tried to further its own cause by allying at expedient times with Lancastrians or Yorkists, so that when Henry Tudor won the battle of Bosworth in 1485 he took charge of an exhausted country. By internal discipline and a wise policy abroad he coaxed back its health and strength in the years that followed. He gathered money wherever he could find it. Rents from royal lands, customs duties, 'gifts' from the Church, heavy fines laid on wealthy offenders, aids for the marriage of his daughter and the knighting of his sons, profitable bargains made with subjects oppressed by the forest laws, payments from gentlemen who declined the expense of knighthood, occasional forced loans, benevolences, and parliamentary grants, all these Henry carefully collected, and even more carefully used. He spent as little as he possibly could. He sometimes threatened war, but he did not wage it. He added half a dozen ships to the Royal Navy and created the Yeomen of the Guard, but he did not maintain a standing army. He kept lucrative offices in royal hands and employed professional deputies to do the work, so that at ten months Prince Henry was created warden of the Cinque Ports and constable of Dover Castle, and at four years old boasted the titles of earl marshal, lord lieutenant of Ireland, and warden of the Scottish Marches. Even when the need for stringent economy had passed, Henry VII could not break his parsimonious habits. He hoarded jewels and plate, cheese-pared court expenses, and left his son a handsome fortune of £1,250,000.

The Marriage of Henry and Catherine

In one respect at least 1509 reminded men of 1485. Within five months of becoming king, Henry VII had married Elizabeth of York, and now, apparently for equally sound political reasons, within two months of his accession, Henry VIII married Catherine, daughter of Ferdinand of Aragon and Isabella of Castile.

Catherine had come to England in October 1501 as the bride-elect of Arthur, Prince of Wales. But, in the following April, to the great sorrow of his father and his young wife, Arthur had died, and left his father and father-in-law with the problem of what to do with the

2 CHARLES V OF SPAIN
*Detail of a contemporary
Flemish portrait*

3 FRANCIS I OF FRANCE
*Detail of a contemporary
portrait*

4   GREENWICH PALACE
Detail of an early seventeenth-century painting

5   RICHMOND PALACE
Engraved by James Basire after 'an ancient drawing'

politically valuable Catherine. Ferdinand did not want to lose England
as a potential ally in his chronic quarrel with France, and Henry valued
the Spanish alliance both as an insurance against diplomatic isolation
in Europe and as a symbol of the new prestige which he had won for
England. Yet neither monarch could resist trying to improve the terms
of their treaty. Ferdinand opened the diplomatic bidding with a
peremptory demand and a contradictory offer, for he instructed his
ambassador, de Puebla, to insist upon Catherine being returned to
Spain with the 100,000 crowns of the half-paid dowry and her widow's
portion of Arthur's estates, and at the same time he let it be known in
London that he was willing to let Catherine marry Prince Henry, the
new heir to the throne. Henry VII had no intention of sending Catherine
back to Spain—still less the dowry or her portion—but he thought it
would be unwise to hasten her marriage to Henry, as yet hardly 11
years of age, and rush into treaty obligations which might well involve
him in expensive war with France. Besides, if in the next few years the
political balance in Western Europe shifted, he might be able to negotiate
an even better marriage for his young son. Letters, some imperious and
others cajoling, passed to and fro between the two courts, while
Catherine and her Spanish household at Durham House in the Strand
idly and impatiently awaited a definite decision.

In June 1503 the negotiations appeared to make a significant advance ✗
when Henry and Catherine were formally betrothed, but in truth
everything remained as tentative as ever. It was agreed that the marriage
could not take place for another three years until after Henry's fifteenth
birthday, but by then Ferdinand must have sent to England the second
half of the dowry, another 100,000 crowns, and the pope must have
granted a dispensation so that Catherine could marry her late husband's
brother. Doña Elvira, the duenna of Catherine's household, stoutly
maintained that Arthur and Catherine had never consummated their
marriage. Ferdinand and Isabella believed her, but in the betrothal
treaty they accepted the natural assumption that Arthur and Catherine
had lived as man and wife during their four-and-a-half months of
married life, and that consequently it was necessary to seek papal
permission for Catherine to marry Henry. Through the death of
Alexander VI and the calculated hesitation of Julius II, the dispensation
was frustratingly slow in coming. But that was not the chief obstacle
in the way of Prince Henry's marriage.

In November 1504 Catherine's mother died. The crown of Castile passed not to her husband but to her daughter, Joanna, and Ferdinand stood in imminent danger of losing control of rich, extensive Castile to his ambitious son-in-law, Philip, the heir to the Holy Roman Empire. Henry VII immediately saw that marriage between Prince Henry and a princess of unimportant Aragon might well be a wasted opportunity. Therefore in the following June, he arranged that his son, not quite 14 years old, should appear before the bishop of Winchester and chosen members of the privy council, and, on grounds of conscience, should protest against the marriage that had been arranged for him. The protest, which was kept semi-secret, did not kill the Anglo-Spanish treaty, but it gave Henry an excuse to seek an alliance with Emperor Maximilian and his son, Philip. Prince Henry might marry Philip's daughter, Eleanor, and Mary might make an excellent match with his son, Charles. It was even possible that Henry VII, who had been a widower since 1503, might himself marry Philip's sister, the twice-widowed Margaret.

Subsequent events induced alternate moods of despair and exhilaration in the hearts of all who were deeply concerned with the betrothal. In the autumn of 1505 Ferdinand sprang a double surprise by coming to terms with Louis XII of France, and frustrating a plan for Henry VII to meet Philip at Calais. But, in the following January, strong winds and high seas drove Philip and Joanna, on their way to Castile, into Melcombe Regis, and thus made possible the signing of a comprehensive treaty between Henry and Philip at Windsor. The prospect of young Henry ever marrying Catherine grew less, despite the fact that in a subsequent letter to Philip, he referred to her as 'my dear and best-loved consort, the princess my wife'. But within six months of leaving Windsor, Philip died. Once more Ferdinand stood supreme in Castile, and when this news reached the English court, Catherine's prospects of marriage revived again.

Time passed. Prince Henry reached his fifteenth birthday, the papal dispensation was at hand, but Ferdinand still failed to send the rest of the dowry to England. Henry quoted this neglect as the obvious reason for delaying the marriage, but it was clear that indecision suited both kings' politics at that time, and that, despite sympathetic words, neither king was prepared to allow the plight of the poverty-stricken and abandoned Catherine to soften his heart or to hurry him into a wrong decision. Partly to silence her complaints and protests, Ferdinand appointed his daughter as his ambassador in England. Within a few months she was urging her father to take up King Henry's suggestion that he should marry her widowed sister, Joanna, for in that project she saw hopes of reviving her own marriage prospects: but early in 1507 she grew alarmed at the reopening of negotiations between England and the Empire. She encouraged Ferdinand to counter-attack. This he did, but he chose as his champion Fuensalida, a touchy, blundering grandee, whom Henry, Bishop Fox, and other councillors had little difficulty in forcing into embarrassing dilemmas and diplo-matic defeats. Meanwhile, Princess Mary had been betrothed to the emperor's grandson, Charles, and through most of 1508 it looked as if England would soon revert to what that generation considered to be the sound tradition of a pro-Burgundian policy. Many political prophets confidently forecast that Prince Henry would soon marry either Charles's sister, Eleanor, or a daughter of the duke of Bavaria. Others, on their guard against accepting what was too obvious, suggested that Henry might suddenly change his diplomatic course altogether, and seal an Anglo-French alliance by marrying his son to Marguerite de Valois, the sister of the future Francis I. Few dared affirm that the Anglo-Spanish treaty would be con-firmed.

Two events quickly transformed the situation—the uniting of France, Spain, and the Empire into the League of Cambrai against Venice in December 1508, and the death of Henry VII in April 1509. Once the League, for the time being, had put an end to the divided Europe which Henry had been trying to exploit, there was no reason why the marriage negotiations should not go ahead. But so long as Henry lived there were barriers in the way. The new king swept them aside with complete disregard for diplomatic caution. He refused to haggle over details of the settlement, and on 11 June 1509, six weeks after his father's elaborate funeral in the unfinished chapel at Westminster and a fortnight before his own coronation in the same abbey, he married Catherine at Greenwich Palace. Ironically, the long years of vacillation and indecision ended in hasty preparations for a quiet wedding solem-nised by Archbishop Warham in the presence of a handful of witnesses. It was commonly believed that Henry was simply fulfilling his dying father's wish by marrying Catherine, but Fuensalida was convinced that he had always wanted to honour the betrothal of 1503, and that this was the first time he had had the freedom to do so. The explanation may be simpler still, for this vigorous young man, comparatively un-acquainted with women at this time, may well have been in love with the petite Catherine, six years his senior. Not for the sake of conven-tional politeness need he have added to a letter to Ferdinand, written on 26 July, that, had he still been free, it would have been Catherine he would have chosen to marry before all other; nor was it in accor-dance with the tradition of the lists that he should wear his wife's favours at the tourneys. With open, boyish eagerness he sought to please Catherine and win her ready praise, and her initial intertwined with his served as a universal decoration at court and proclaimed his joy in his marriage. Catherine wrote to her father that it was her obedience to his will that moved her to love Henry, but clearly she too was overjoyed at the marriage. To be the queen of so handsome and popular a king, to be the centre of so gay and lively a court, to be set free so suddenly and unexpectedly from the gloom, boredom, anxiety, and poverty of her life at Durham House could not have failed to enrapture and amaze her.

The New Régime

During his father's lifetime, Henry VIII lived a semi-secluded life devoted to his studies and his sport. He received a good grounding in the etiquette of formal occasions and in the nature of sovereignty, but not in the art of government or in the conduct of foreign affairs. He took up the crown with confidence. He felt himself 'every inch a king', and from the first demanded full recognition of his status and his un-limited authority. But it is difficult to assess his opinion of his father's policy. During the first few months of his reign he sometimes reacted strongly against it, and sometimes followed it sedulously. On the one hand, he showed none of his father's diplomatic finesse, and made no attempt to hide his feelings or to disguise his intentions. Without any inhibitions he flung himself into the life of a gay, roistering, splendidly dressed court, tirelessly feasting, hunting, jousting, dancing, and revelling at Greenwich, Westminster, and Richmond. Henry himself wrote and sang verses which could well serve as the motto of these early days.

Pastime with good company
I love and shall until I die
Grudge who will, but none deny,
So God be pleased this life will I
For my pastime,
Hunt, sing, and dance,
My heart is set;
All goodly sport
To my comfort
Who shall me let?

The king and queen, as well as the wealthy young men they attracted to court, spent money with what seemed reckless abandon after the parsimony of Henry VII. Their staff-wages bill lengthened alarmingly; open-handed giving and constant entertainment replaced hoarding and a carefully regulated court. On the other hand, Henry made no major changes in his father's council, and he contentedly left it to regulate routine affairs, and to advise him on matters which did not touch him personally. One of his first official acts was to confirm his father's promise to redress grievances, and to order the imprisonment of Sir Richard Empson and Edmund Dudley, the two executives chiefly associated with carrying out Henry VII's policy of impoverishing wealthy subjects in order to enrich his crown. No other act could have been more popular, and probably because it met with such widespread approval and increased his own popularity, Henry did not hesitate to accept his councillors' advice that, since justifiable charges of extortion would seem to condemn his father more than Empson and Dudley, they should be tried on a trumped-up charge of treason. If he thought about it seriously at all, Henry probably considered the contrived execution of two hated servants a small price to pay for keeping his father's name free from further blemish, and for increasing his own reputation for generosity and liberality at the same time. And Archbishop Warham, the chancellor, and Bishops Fox and Ruthal, lord privy seal and secretary respectively, had good reason to be glad if the sacrifice of Empson and Dudley quietened a potentially dangerous outcry against recent injustices.

Happily, Catherine had no need to pretend that she enjoyed sharing her husband's pleasures and conversation. She had a genuine enthusiasm for hunting and jousting, appreciated music and good craftsmanship, loved to discuss books and theology, and held the same views as Henry

about the responsibilities and authority which a crown imposed upon
its wearer. Whatever subject was uppermost in his mind, Henry could
be sure of finding in his wife an informed and interested listener. Four
months after her wedding Catherine knew that she was pregnant. This
was joyful news indeed, for the birth of an heir would set the seal on the
king's happiness. Throughout the winter Henry took great care that
Catherine should not run any physical risks, but in the spring he had
to bear the disappointment of a still-born daughter. Such blows of
fortune were considered to be so natural and inevitable in the sixteenth
century that Henry could not have grieved unduly, especially as
Catherine became pregnant again soon afterwards. At Richmond on
1 January 1511 she gave birth to a prince. The happy king celebrated
his fatherhood with a pilgrimage to Walsingham and an elaborate
pageant at Westminster. Edward Hall described the riotous festivities
and unbridled rejoicings which were conducted 'with myrth and
gladnes', but the memory of them soon afterwards mocked all who had
taken part. For on 22 February the baby unaccountably sickened and
died.

> The kyng lyke a wyse Prynce, took this dolorous chaunce wonderous
> wysely, and the more to comfort the Quene, he dissimuled the matter, and
> made no great mourning outwardely: but the Quene lyke a naturall woman,
> made muche lamentacion, how be it, by the kynges good persuasion and
> behaviour, her sorrow was mytigated, but not shortlye.

Henry's Diplomatic Apprenticeship

Erasmus condemned war-mongering kings for 'pouncing like
ravenous birds' on mankind's wealth and knowledge, and Colet
affirmed that 'an unjust peace is better than the most just of wars', but
most of their contemporaries considered it natural and commendable
that a young, lusty, and wealthy king should have martial ambitions.
It is true that, in the early sixteenth century, war was not so compulsive
and automatic a royal policy as it had been a century before in the reign
of Henry V, but Henry VIII would have been strangely out of his
generation, if, at 18, he had been content to follow his father's careful,
peaceful policy indefinitely without once being eager to try his fortune
on the battlefield. Not that he knew anything about waging war: he

was moved partly by a guileless determination to use England's might on the side of right in Europe, and largely by ambition and desire for adventure. 'The gay lilied fields of France', made more romantic by imaginative idealised accounts of Crécy and Agincourt, he could not easily banish from his mind. He saw war as a gigantic tournament, in which French men-at-arms, despite their greater numbers, were usually worsted by English noblemen, and routed by the native skill of English archers. He was innocently ignorant of the fire-power and the new skills of the professional armies then fighting on the Continent.

Henry VII had not entangled himself in the dangerous and profitless confusion of Italian politics, but Ferdinand, with his hold on Naples and his ambitions in Northern Italy, could not help but become heavily and constantly involved. He now hoped to use his new son-in-law as an ally, and through Catherine in the early months of their marriage, he put before Henry his version of events. Henry showed lively interest. Hardly had he become king before he was denouncing the injustice of the League of Cambrai against Venice, and attempting to champion the republic. He was puzzled that the pope had approved so wicked a conspiracy, and that Maximilian and Ferdinand were apparently blind to the danger of encouraging France. It was, however, not Henry's protest but the French victory at Agnadello that saved Venice, for it made Julius II so frightened of French domination in northern Italy that he began to demolish the League of Cambrai and build an anti-French alliance. The outcome was the Holy League formed between Emperor Maximilian, Ferdinand, and the papacy in October 1511. This was more to Henry's liking—and to Catherine's. Both rejoiced at the prospect of being 'the Paladin of the Church', and therefore automatically on the side of moral right, and both were happy to think of being allied with Ferdinand and opposed to Louis XII, who recently had incriminated himself further in Henry's eyes by trying to depose the pope. In November, Henry eagerly accepted Julius's invitation to join the alliance, and he undertook to attack France in the following spring. Warham and Fox still counselled caution and peace: Surrey who, curiously enough, held the post of treasurer, advised action. Parliament met in February 1512. Henry informed both houses that the papacy was in danger and appealing for help. The commons dutifully voted money, and preparations for war went smoothly ahead.

The next two years taught Henry something of the difficulties of war and the reality of diplomacy. He joined the Holy League confident that he was supporting good against evil, proud of his allies, and unafraid of the outcome; he emerged from it far more sceptical of the moral leadership of Rome, angry with Ferdinand and Maximilian, partially cured of romantic pictures of English empires in Europe, and determined to be less trusting of others and more regardful of himself in future. Not that the campaign was all loss—on the contrary.

Early in April 1512, as good as his word, Henry sent his fleet into the Channel to attack French shipping and threaten French ports, and for the next twelve months his admiral, Sir Edward Howard, kept up what pressure he could with his small number of ships. In June, 10,000 English troops, mostly archers and led by the marquis of Dorset, landed at Fuenterrabia at the western end of the Pyrenees. Henry sent them there at the advice and request of Ferdinand, who, through Catherine, had carefully nurtured the hope that they would reconquer Guienne and restore English rule in south-west France. But Ferdinand failed to provide Dorset with the cavalry, artillery, and transport he had promised, and before the end of the year Henry's proud army straggled back home fever-ridden and dishonoured. Dorset had not even managed to attack Bayonne, the nearest of Guienne's garrison towns, but the very presence of his army so near the French frontier had held down French troops and made it easier for Ferdinand's troops to take Navarre and give Castile and Aragon a strong defensive bastion to the north-west. This first lesson in international politics was lost on Henry. He bitterly resented the damage done to his military prestige, but he accepted Ferdinand's glib explanations without question. He held the unfortunate Dorset solely responsible for the disaster. So determined was he to wipe out the disgraceful memory of Fuenterrabia that he gladly fell in with his father-in-law's plans for the next campaigning season. Warham and other councillors who had served Henry VII advised the king against throwing good money after bad, but Henry undertook to send Ferdinand 100,000 crowns so that Spain could hire mercenaries to invade Guienne, arranged to have Howard continue his hostilities in the Channel, and agreed that he himself should lead an army into northern France.

He laid his invasion plans carefully and elaborately. Since the late summer of 1512 he had had a small force under Surrey keeping an eye on the Scottish border and arranging for the mobilisation of the northern shire-musters should the Scots threaten to intervene on the side of France. He watched as closely as he could the comings and goings between the courts of Scotland and France, and goaded Howard into such desperate energy at sea that in April 1513, he was defeated and killed in trying to carry out a hopeless mission off Brest. In that same month Henry answered the latest appeal from Rome by pledging himself to declare war on France within the next four weeks. The Emperor Maximilian and Ferdinand of Aragon made the same promise, but Maximilian had no means to make it effective, and, only four days previously, after negotiations which had lasted several months, Ferdinand had signed a year's truce with Louis XII. Henry heard of this truce, which applied everywhere but Italy, before his army left England, but he and Catherine believed Ferdinand's complicated and confused story that Caroz, the Spanish ambassador in England, had clumsily or wickedly deceived both courts. Henry shut his mind to the thought that Ferdinand had once again cynically used England for Spanish purposes, and he was so wholeheartedly involved in his preparations for re-establishing the reputation of English arms, that whatever news came from Europe it would have been difficult for him to think of cancelling the invasion. Before he left for France, Henry took the precaution of executing the imprisoned Edmund de la Pole, earl of Suffolk. The charge, treasonable correspondence with his brother across the Channel, merely masked Henry's fear that, during his absence from England, some disaffected subjects might plot to put Suffolk on the throne. It was an outside chance at best, but with a remedy so readily at hand, Henry saw no reason for running the risk.

The English army crossed to Calais in three parts. The spearhead, some 8000 men, served under the earl of Shrewsbury, the second wave, a slightly smaller force, under Lord Herbert, and the main army, 11,000 men carried in 400 ships, under King Henry himself. This intimidating host, three times the size of Henry V's victorious army, was magnificently apparelled and fully equipped—or hampered— with spare horses, elaborate tents, standards, heraldic emblems, and all the secondary requirements for war. It made a brave, colourful show, and with it Henry besieged the little but strongly fortified town of Thérouanne, not far from St. Omer, from mid-June until late August.

Such a formidable army forcing so late a surrender could hardly claim exceptional success, and the driving away of a relieving column of cavalry on 16 August 1513—the Battle of the Spurs—did not merit the jubilation which followed it. From Thérouanne Henry dragged his equipment 50 miles further inland to besiege Tournai, and after a second surrender he returned first to Calais and thence to England, gratified that his expedition had been successful and confident that he had restored prestige to English arms. But if anyone had done that it was not Henry but Surrey, whose northern army at Flodden early in September had destroyed the Scottish army which James IV had led across the border in an attempt to relieve the pressure on his ally, Louis of France. James himself lay dead among his nobles. The new king, a child 18 months old, was Henry's nephew.

Emperor Maximilian met Henry during the siege of Thérouanne. He came mock-humbly, without any forces, and flattered Henry by nominally serving under his command. But by persuading the English to attack Tournai and pay for the hire of German mercenaries he gained what he could from the campaign, and then at Lille in October, agreed that Henry, Ferdinand and he should reopen the attack on France in the following summer. Henry drew attention to the treaty of 1508 which had arranged for Princess Mary to marry Archduke Charles when Charles was 14 years old—that is, within the following year—and Maximilian gave his word that the marriage should take place before 15 May 1514. Henry's victorious homecoming was marred by an outbreak of plague in London and the news of Catherine's second miscarriage: in February his own illness, measles or small-pox, slowed down his preparation for the coming campaign of which he had extravagant hopes. But by March he was well again, as eager and as ebullient as ever. It was soon clear, however, that something had gone wrong with the agreement reached at Lille. The Spanish ambassador insisted that he had no instructions from Ferdinand to ratify the Anglo-Spanish alliance, and obviously Maximilian had done nothing to arrange the marriage of Charles and Mary. Indeed, unknown to Henry, both had spent the winter trying to patch up a treaty with France, and in April, to his great wrath, Henry heard from Paris that Ferdinand had come to terms with Louis about the Pyrenean frontier. When he learned that Maximilian, to whom he had given considerable funds for the war, was also seeking a truce with France, Henry's disillusionment was complete. Even the new pope, Leo X, did not want war. Henry saw himself isolated in Europe, all because, he declared, he alone had stood by his word. He was angry, but not dismayed or helpless. With supreme self-confidence he told the Venetian ambassador, 'I do not see any faith in the world save in me only, and therefore God Almighty, who knows this, prospers my affairs.'

Twelve months earlier Henry would probably have felt obliged to fulfil his signed obligations whatever his allies chose to do. Even now he took care not to do anything definite until after 15 May, so that the emperor and his friends could not accuse him of wrecking the Lille treaty. But the duplicity of others made him resolve to look after his own interests. He had no wish to waste his wealth on a single-handed war with France. That was far too serious and suicidal a prospect. If he could not join an effective anti-French alliance, then he might come to terms with Louis, who without question would value either his help or, better still, his neutrality. Peace was not unattractive, for war, he had discovered, ate money and took all his attention. And Scotland, with his sister Margaret as regent, held out interesting possibilities for exploitation. Therefore, contrary to his previous policy and without protest from Catherine, who seems to have been as disgusted with Ferdinand as her husband was, Henry approached Louis, and by 10 August instead of being in the middle of another expensive and largely futile campaign, he had signed a peace treaty. In exchange for England's neutrality in Europe, Louis agreed to pay Henry a handsome pension and allow him to keep Tournai. The seal on the bargain was that the youthful Princess Mary should marry the elderly Louis XII. This diplomatic somersault gave Henry as much satisfaction as his military victories in the previous year. He had defeated Ferdinand and Maximilian at their own game, and he was confident that he now had a far clearer idea of how to go adventuring in Europe. Two things increased his satisfaction—Catherine was expecting another child before the end of the year, and he believed he had found a clever, agreeable minister of his own, not one of his father's choice, in Thomas Wolsey. In December he suffered a grievous disappointment when his second son died within a few hours of birth, but he felt more and more confident that his new minister would serve him well.

Wolsey's Early Career

Thomas Wolsey was a precocious boy. He was the son of an Ipswich butcher—

> *He came of the sang royall*
> *That was cast out of a butcher's stall*

scoffed his enemy Skelton—but his father had sufficient money and interest in his education to send him to Magdalen College, Oxford. Before he was 20 years old, young Thomas graduated, gained a fellowship of his college, served as bursar and as master of Magdalen College School, and, as absentee priest, received stipends from at least three parishes. In 1501, his twentieth year, he left Oxford to become domestic chaplain first, for a couple of years, to Henry Deane, archbishop of Canterbury, and then to Sir Richard Nanfan, the deputy governor of Calais. Nanfan died in 1507, but Wolsey was fortunate enough to be appointed one of the royal chaplains, and to be used occasionally by Henry VII for lesser diplomatic work. Wolsey was no pious, dedicated priest. Through church preferment he hoped to increase his wealth and authority, but his true interest and ability lay in secular affairs.

When Henry VII died, Wolsey lost the third powerful patron he had had since he left Oxford eight years previously. He still enjoyed the patronage of Richard Mayewe, president of Magdalen and bishop of Hereford, from whom he received the office of dean of Hereford in 1509, but obviously the most desirable patron in England was the new king. Thanks to the good offices of Fox, Henry VIII appointed Wolsey his almoner during the first months of his reign. He thus gave this ambitious priest a precarious foothold on the royal band-wagon. In the next five years he was to see him elbow and slide his way into the conductor's seat.

Henry VIII had no liking for tedious administrative matters, which stole precious hours he much preferred to give to riding, music, merrymaking, and other congenial activities. In his first few months as king, he left as much administration as he could to his father's councillors, Warham, Fox, and Ruthal, but from 1510 onwards, he, or they, relied increasingly upon his new almoner. Certainly the disillusioned and angry mutineers who deserted the marquis of Dorset at Fuenterrabia in 1512 considered Wolsey to be the chief cause of their disgrace and distress. Luckily for Wolsey, Henry blamed the unfortunate Dorset, but Wolsey knew that he dared not risk being associated with a second disaster. To ensure the success of the 1513 campaign he worked resolutely and long. He ordered supplies, requisitioned shipping, arranged for sufficient ready money to be at hand, crossed to Calais with Henry's party, and during the fighting and subsequent negotiations held himself always ready to serve and advise the king. He spent as much time with Henry as did Charles Brandon, the king's favourite jousting companion. He it was who persuaded Henry that he must be as self-seeking as Maximilian and Ferdinand, and he who guided him into the truce with Louis in 1514. Modesty did not cloud his vision of his influence at court. He told the Venetian ambassador, 'As I was the author of the peace, so I will exert myself to confirm and preserve it.' His most direct reward was to be elevated to the sees of Lincoln and Tournai, but his soundest gain was the winning of Henry's confidence. From this time onwards, the king dispensed with the small administrative council he had been using. He listened to Wolsey's advice on all major matters; usually, but not always, accepted it; and then left it to Wolsey to see that the royal will was put into effect. Since no other councillor had the ear of the king and since Henry attended to matters of state only in energetic fits and starts, the reality of temporal power in England now lay with efficient, hard-working Wolsey. He did not hesitate to interpret his authority widely.

At the same time Wolsey was planning to control ecclesiastical England. Bainbridge, cardinal-archbishop of York, died in Rome in July 1514. He timed his death so conveniently for Wolsey's preferment that contemporaries accused Silvester de Giglis, bishop of Worcester and friend of Wolsey, of poisoning him. But Warham, though he yielded the lord chancellorship to Wolsey in 1515, disobligingly lived on as archbishop of Canterbury, and thus confined Wolsey to the see of York. To overcome Warham's senior authority, Wolsey sought to persuade Leo X to create him a permanent special legate, *legatus a latere*. Early in 1514, Polydore Vergil, the chronicler, and Silvester de Giglis, both under Wolsey's instructions but knowing nothing of the other's mission, were each pleading Wolsey's advancement in Rome. After arranging the peace treaty with France, Wolsey requested the help of Louis XII, and on 12 August 1514 Henry wrote privately to Leo asking him to create Wolsey, 'our most secret counsellor', a cardinal. The

pope allowed a decent interval to pass, and then, in 1515, admitted
Wolsey to the college of cardinals. Three years later, he invested him
with the extraordinary powers of *legatus a latere*, and for the next
decade, under the distant authority of Rome and with Henry's trust
and consent, Wolsey ruled England in church and state.

The wedding of Louis XII and Princess Mary proclaimed Wolsey's
first major diplomatic success. Unfortunately for him, but fortunately
for Mary, the marriage was short-lived. Louis died on 1 January 1515,
hastened to his grave, men thought, by trying to keep pace with his
active and gay young wife. His heir was his nephew, Francis I, ambitious,
vigorous, if not too handsome, and it would probably have pleased
Henry and Wolsey, and probably Francis himself, if he had married the
widowed queen. But Mary had other plans. She had not married Louis
willingly, but had been persuaded to do so partly by his short expectation of life, and partly by Henry's promise that when she married again,
she should marry as she 'liketh for to do'. Whoever else had forgotten
that promise, Mary had not. Others might speculate about the advantages of her marrying Francis or Charles of the Netherlands, but she
had set her heart on Charles Brandon, boisterous, brawny, and recently
created duke of Suffolk. Brandon had a reputation as a lady-killer.
Three ladies already claimed to be his wife in law or in practice. But
that did not deter Mary. As soon as he arrived in Paris, where, somewhat imprudently, Henry had sent him to escort her to England, she
urged him to marry her immediately. Brandon hesitated, if only
because he had undertaken to bring her back to England as a widow.
To marry Henry's sister without Henry's knowledge and consent
might easily be suicidal. But Mary insisted, Francis encouraged, and
eventually Brandon agreed. Apprehension followed. Wolsey wrote
that Henry had received the news 'grievously and displeasantly', but
that Suffolk had a slim chance of earning a pardon if he persuaded
Francis to return Mary's dowry, plate, and jewels to Henry. This,
surprisingly enough, Suffolk managed to do. Francis probably thought
it was a fair price to pay to have Suffolk as an ally in the English court,
but whether the gold and the jewels did soften Henry's heart it is
difficult to say. Wolsey claimed that it was he who persuaded Henry to
forgive: others gave Catherine the credit. But it may well be that
Henry's heart required little softening, for Mary was a beloved sister
and Suffolk a boon companion. On their return to England, Henry did

6 CARDINAL WOLSEY
Detail of a contemporary portrait by an unknown artist

7 ARCHBISHOP WARHAM
Detail of the drawing by Hans Holbein; reproduced by gracious permission of H.M. The Queen

8 CATHERINE OF ARAGON (1509)
Detail of a portrait by Meister Michael

9 ANNE BOLEYN (1533)
Detail of the drawing by Hans Holbein

10 JANE SEYMOUR (1536)
*Detail of the drawing by Hans Holbein;
reproduced by gracious permission of H.M.
The Queen*

11 ANNE OF CLEVES (1540)
Detail of a contemporary German portrait

12 CATHERINE HOWARD (1540)
*Detail of a contemporary miniature; repro-
duced by gracious permission of H.M. The
Queen*

13 CATHERINE PARR (1543)
Detail of an anonymous portrait

HENRY VIII's WIVES

not send Brandon to the Tower nor compel Mary to carry out her threat of going to a nunnery to escape another diplomatic marriage. Instead, he and his court witnessed a second wedding ceremony at Greenwich, and both Mary and Suffolk remained in the royal favour. True it was that Suffolk did not share Henry's companionship as constantly as he had previously done, but he found ample compensation in his vivacious wife and in his new home in the country. He could also draw some satisfaction from his successful defiance of the strict convention which reserved royal ladies for princes and kings, though, were he wise, he would always heed the injunction of a contemporary,

Cloth of frize, be not too bold,
Tho' thou be matched with cloth of gold.

Henry and Francis

The coming of Francis I to the French throne evoked as much joy and expectation in Paris as Henry's accession had done in London six years earlier. Henry burned with curiosity. He invited a company of Venetians to Greenwich for the May Day festivities of 1515, took one of them aside and asked, 'The king of France, is he as tall as I am? Is he stout? What sort of legs has he?' For Henry was as vain as any woman. Constantly he delighted in wearing the most expensive clothes and being attended by beautifully dressed courtiers and by servants in extravagant liveries. He set out to impress these shrewd Venetians, who had come to England through France, and later would be voicing their opinions throughout Europe. They must leave England convinced that neither the English court nor the English king was one whit inferior to the court and person of Francis I. Already, in March at Richmond, he had received them most impressively, with carefully staged, Mussolini-like devices for securing the maximum dramatic effect. Their reports show how their favourable verdict on the English court was shaped by the magnificent royal barge which brought them up river, by the tall halberdiers, by the numerous noblemen and clergy in attendance, but mostly by Henry himself, dressed in gold, white, and crimson, wearing two gold collars ornamented with diamonds, and with his fingers thick with jewelled rings. Now, on May morning, the king showed them the English court in a different mood. He had dressed from head to foot in green to attend an early, outdoor breakfast of venison prepared by 'Robin Hood and his outlaws'. Singers, courtiers, green-clad soldiers, and all the cardboard *grotesquerie* of carnival formed a procession along the lanes and into the woods. The breakfast was a sumptuous feast, but, later in the day, these frivolities were dwarfed in importance by a three-hour tourney, in which Henry led Suffolk, Dorset, Essex and other nobles through no less than thirty courses. Francis might be a younger man and king of a richer land, but Henry seemed determined he would not steal his reputation of being the gayest and most athletic monarch in Europe.

Throughout 1515 Henry did not find it easy to put France out of his mind, for Francis was full of surprises. At the same time that he was renewing the Anglo-French treaty of friendship, he was encouraging John Stewart, duke of Albany, to go to Scotland and oppose the regency of Henry's sister, Margaret. Francis argued that trouble between England and Scotland would guarantee Henry's inaction in Europe better than his seal on a formal treaty. Albany was most successful: by September, Henry found himself with Margaret and her second husband, the earl of Angus, on his hands as refugees. On the Continent Francis came to an understanding with young Charles of the Netherlands, and then surprised everyone by rapidly crossing the Alps in September and defeating Sforza's troops and his Swiss allies at Marignano, a dozen miles to the south-east of Milan. This lightning campaign shattered the precarious settlement which had been reached in Italy the previous year, and piled more trouble on the aged shoulders of Maximilian and Ferdinand. Francis exploited his victory by making peace with the Swiss, and, at Bologna, agreeing with Leo X that French-controlled Milan should recover Parma and Piacenza, and that, as king, he should henceforward nominate the archbishops and bishops of France.

September 1515, therefore, was a black month for English interests abroad. Through his ambassadors in London, Ferdinand eagerly urged that the enemies of France should again take up arms against her, but Henry and Wolsey remembered the disastrous expedition to Fuenterrabia and the cost of the Thérouanne-Tournai campaign, and consequently negotiated with caution. They refused to go to war, but in October agreed to hire 20,000 Swiss mercenaries to help Maximilian recover Milan. The commons declined to vote all the money Henry asked for, and Cuthbert Tunstal echoed the thoughts in many men's

minds when, a few weeks later, he wrote to Wolsey from the Netherlands, 'I do not see why at this time our master should . . . bind himself
to maintain other men's causes, wherein they themselves be so dull.'
Warham resigned the chancellorship and Fox the privy seal, but
opposition and argument did not hold back Henry and Wolsey from
fulfilling the agreement. Richard Pace, the king's new secretary, raised
the troops in Switzerland, and, in March 1516, as soon as it was possible
to campaign again, Maximilian led them across the Swiss frontier into
the Milanese. Three days later, without a reasonable cause and without
having struck a solitary blow, the emperor abandoned the campaign and
retreated into Switzerland. Henry's hard-begotten money had all been
wasted. To make matters worse, Francis soon afterwards manœuvred
Charles of the Netherlands, the young heir of Ferdinand who had died
in January 1516, into signing an unfortunate treaty at Noyon. Only
Henry and the unreliable, impecunious Maximilian now opposed
France and French supremacy in Europe. Foolishly, Henry again sent
money to his ally, this time so that he could march to Brussels and
persuade his grandson, Charles, to desert the French. As might have
been expected, Maximilian proved as faithless as ever. Instead of
destroying the Treaty of Noyon, he accepted a French bribe and
became a partner in it in January 1517. Two months later he confirmed
this by signing a treaty with Francis and Charles for a new division of
Italy. Henry stood outside these negotiations, uninvited and ignored.
Even he had to realise that Francis had won the first round.

2 HENRY AND WOLSEY

Why come ye not to court?
To whiche court?
To the kinges court
Or to Hampton Court?

JOHN SKELTON

HENRY did not take these diplomatic reverses too much to heart. News of Marignano and of Maximilian's retreat sent him into towering rages, but when he calmed down he put his trust in Wolsey, and Wolsey trusted time and diplomacy rather than arms. Besides, in Henry's life there were important things other than foreign affairs. On 18 February 1516, at Greenwich Palace, Queen Catherine gave birth to a daughter, Mary. This time the child was healthy enough, and, as Henry declared, 'We are both young: if it was a daughter this time, by the grace of God the sons will follow.' Far from showing disappointment in the baby's sex, Henry doted on her extravagantly. He displayed her to the court, his eyes radiant with pride, and solemnly assured the Venetian ambassador that she never cried! Catherine, 30 years old when Mary was born, had been so weakened by her several pregnancies that she found it impossible to keep pace with Henry's tireless energy. The king's physical vigour was at its peak: in his middle twenties he was a fine-looking man. Pasqualigo, the Venetian ambassador in London, wrote at this time that Henry was the most handsome ruler he had ever set eyes on. He stood upright and tall, with a fair complexion and bright auburn hair 'combed straight and short in the French fashion'. His face was round, his throat rather long and thick, and he had a stout calf to his leg. Out of these April days of young manhood and bodily perfection, he was determined to take all the pleasure he could find.

The gay, vigorous court life went on without end. Constantly,

34

Henry hunted with hawk or hound, and, in addition to the customary festivals, seized any excuse for staging a joust or a pageant, or for giving a banquet, a concert, or a ball. Ingenious and ingenuous devices abounded, for Henry and the younger courtiers never seemed to tire of disguising themselves as dancers, outlaws, and strange knights in order to 'surprise' the ladies at the appropriate moment. In May 1516 two 'solempne dates of Justes' marked the arrival of Queen Margaret of Scotland at Greenwich. On the first day, Henry, Suffolk, Essex, and Nicholas Carew, one of Henry's favourite companions for japes and carnivals, all dressed in black velvet 'covered al over with braunches of hony suckels of fine flat gold of dammaske, of lose worke, every lefe of the braunche moving', jousted throughout the day against numerous opponents. '. . . every man did well, but the kyng did best, and so was adjudged, and so at night they ceased, and came to supper'. The second day Henry and his companions wore purple velvet, 'set ful of leaves of clothe of gold, engrailed with fyne flat golde of dammaske, embroudered like to Rose leves'. Again they jousted spectacularly: after Henry had unhorsed the strong and tall Sir William Kingston, he and his friends 'ranne volant at all commers, whiche was a plesaunt sight to se'. The day ended with 'a great banket for the welcome of the quene of Scottes'.

When ceremony or etiquette required it, Henry rarely failed to have Catherine by his side, but he often found younger ladies than the queen to amuse him, and occasionally to consort with him. Since the Christmas festivities of 1514 he had been particularly fond of Elizabeth Blount, one of Catherine's ladies-in-waiting, indefatigable in court romps and merry-making. With a perspicacity probably born of after events, Hall wrote that this blonde girl, the daughter of Sir John Blount of Kinlet in Shropshire and a kinswoman of Lord Mountjoy, exceeded all others at court in singing, dancing, and 'all goodly pastymes'; and, writing in the middle of the seventeenth century, Lord Herbert of Cherbury used the curious expression that she 'was thought for her rare ornaments of nature and education to be the mistress-piece of her time'. By 1518, the court openly recognised her as the king's favourite mistress, and, in the spring of 1519, she retired to the Priory of St. Lawrence at Blackmore, Essex, to bear him a son. Henry did not flaunt Bessie's success before Catherine; still less did he allow Catherine's dignity as queen to be slighted or ignored. But he openly showed his pleasure in the young mother and her baby. He had the child christened Henry Fitzroy, and both he and Wolsey, the boy's godfather, saw to it that Mistress Blount and infant Henry received the respect to which the fatherhood of the child entitled them.

Just as the noisy, jaunty, and carefree behaviour of apprentices, students, and young service-men does not preclude serious application to their work, so Henry's love of physical pleasures did not prevent him from taking his royal responsibilities seriously. One cannot dismiss him as an extravagant, dissolute profligate. He gloried in the strength of his young limbs, he enjoyed food and drink, he liked colour, a trim figure, and a pretty face, and he delighted in being the central figure of a ceremony, a dance, or a joust, and hearing gasps of astonishment when the crowds saw how splendidly he carried himself, and rounds of applause when he played the lute or overthrew his opponent in the lists. But he was ever the king, the head of state alone responsible for the suppression of evil and for the safety and well-being of his people.

Throughout his life, Henry took a deep interest in naval matters. Like his father, and unlike some of his ministers including Wolsey, he appreciated the national importance of defending English merchant ships and English ports against French attack, and was prepared to meet the expense. He did not abandon the time-honoured practice of commissioning merchant ships when the military situation required it, but he gradually increased Henry VII's small fleet of royal ships which were designed and equipped only for war. In the first two years of his reign he built *Mary Rose* of 600 tons and *Peter Pomegranate* of 450 tons. In 1512, after the news that his father's crack ship, *Regent*, had been burnt out in action with the French ship, *Cordelière*, off Brest, Henry 'caused a great shippe to be made, such another as was never seen before in England, and called it *Henry grâce de Dieu*'. It was a carrack, with massive forecastle and high poop, armed with 120 small guns, and boasting a displacement of over 1000 tons. Yet for all the pride its impressive appearance evoked in Englishmen, there was no denying that it was difficult to steer, and that in roughish weather it rolled alarmingly. When his warships were not in action, Henry had them either in the anchorages which he had improved along the south coast, or in the greater safety of the royal 'dockyards', which he founded at Deptford and Woolwich. In May 1514, he granted a group of Deptford sailors permission to form a Guild of Holy Trinity and St. Clement pledged to improve, by pilots, buoys, lights and other means, the safety of navigation in the Thames and its approaches. In the last year of Henry's reign, this guild changed its name to the more familiar Corporation of Trinity House.

Henry did not leave these matters to his councillors or his servants. He wanted to see everything for himself. He watched his ships at manœuvres, and studied such technical matters as the construction of hulls, the ranges of different types of guns, and the siting of coastal defences. When his ships sailed for Fuenterrabia in 1512 and for Brest in 1513, he was at the port to see them off, and early in November 1515, he gave a dinner party on board his latest pride, a great galley driven by 120 oars, armed by more than 200 small guns, and capable of carrying 1000 troops. After the bishop of Durham had said Mass, Queen Catherine named the galley *Princess Mary*, but naturally Henry himself had to steal the show by displaying his skill and knowledge before his admiring friends. He dressed as a sailor— except that few other sailors wore clothes made of cloth of gold—and in the grand manner captained the vessel on its short maiden voyage on the Thames. From a gold chain round his neck hung the whistle which was the usual symbol of command on board, and Henry 'blew [it] nearly as loud as a trumpet'.

On horseback or in the council chamber, Henry knew neither danger nor hesitation, but news of epidemics drove away his confidence. There was good reason for fear, for epidemics attacked the young and healthy as frequently as the old and infirm. Medical science stood powerless, and many of the king's friends, including his brother, Arthur, and his Latin secretary, Andreas Ammonius, had been plague victims. 'This malady', wrote Hall, 'was so cruell that it killed some within three hours, some within twoo houres, some mery at diner and dedde at supper.' In 1517 and 1518 sweating sickness followed by plague attacked London with unusual ferocity. 'We are in the greatest sorrow and danger', wrote Thomas More to Erasmus in August 1517. 'Many are dying all round us; almost everyone in Oxford, Cambridge, and London has been ill lately, and many of our best and most honoured friends have perished.' From London Henry retreated first to Windsor then to Abingdon, Greenwich, Richmond, and Esher, moving around from place to place in an attempt to have as little contact as possible between the court and the plague-stricken areas. Court life was reduced to a bare routine. Christmas and other festivals went by uncelebrated, and Henry whiled away much of his leisure time playing and listening to music. For most of these months of wandering, Henry had with him a skilled organist, a Venetian friar, whom he had appointed chaplain and choirmaster in 1516. He spent hours listening to his playing, and, according to the Venetian ambassador, 'had a greater opinion of him than words can express'. To Henry music was a constant delight and solace. He was always ready to try new instruments, or to engage and listen to singers, organists, clavichord and lute players, whose skill he knew from experience or whose playing he had heard praised by others. He and Wolsey, as well as their choirmasters, Cornish and Pigott, enjoyed a friendly rivalry over their chapel choirs. At Easter 1518, Henry delightedly received at Abingdon a boy soloist from Wolsey's choir. He bade Cornish treat him kindly, 'otherwise than he doth his own', and, in turn, Cornish generously praised the lad and his teacher for his 'sure and clearly singing' and 'for his good and crafty descant'. This was praise indeed, for several contemporaries echoed the opinion of the Venetian secretary, who, in a private letter, declared that the voices of the royal choristers were divine rather than human.

Though Henry and his 'slenderly furnished' court managed to live out of London for many months, Wolsey had to stay in London to transact government business. He did not escape the sickness: for weeks in the autumn of 1517, he struggled against the weakness which followed two attacks of sweating sickness within three months. Necessity goaded him on, for Henry's absence from London left even more work than usual in his hands. Apart from an easy-going treasurer, the duke of Norfolk, and a docile privy seal, Ruthal, Wolsey had no one with whom he could discuss problems on terms of equal or comparable responsibility. Not that he resented his isolation. In his first years as lord chancellor and chief minister, his hard work in the courts, in the details of financial administration, in attempts to improve trade and agriculture, and in diplomatic negotiations, all strengthened his influence in government and made him indispensable to the king. Occasionally he had to leave London to seek an audience with Henry, in order to keep him informed of policy developments or to obtain a ruling. On one occasion he reversed the process, and brought Henry to London as a *deus ex machina* to settle serious disorders in the city. From Eastertide 1517 the London apprentices had been particularly hostile to foreigners living in the capital. Norfolk and his son, the earl of Surrey, marched a small army of retainers into London, and so brutally handled a hostile demonstration of apprentices on the eve of May Day, that the whole city seethed with anger. A deputation of aldermen went to Greenwich to lay their grievances before the king. Henry referred them to Wolsey, but almost a fortnight later, at Wolsey's express request, he ventured the hazards of the plague and sat in Westminster Hall to hear the charges against the apprentices. Wolsey had the hearing carefully staged to produce the maximum tension and, ultimately, the greatest relief. Four hundred prisoners, each with a rope around his neck, shuffled into ranks in front of the dais. Their unkempt condition after days in gaol contrasted harshly with the magnificence of Henry's nobles and councillors, and with the colour and dignity of the mayor and aldermen 'in their best livery according as the Cardinall had them apoynted'. After evidence had been given, despite the tearful pleading of Queen Catherine, Henry condemned all the prisoners to the gallows. But, as had been arranged, Wolsey fell on his knees before the throne, and by last-minute pleading won from Henry a grudging pardon. The prisoners' joy quickly spread through the city, affection for the crown increased, and Wolsey gained respect and awe. But Londoners could still not understand Henry's tolerant and favourable treatment of foreign merchants, clerics, and scholars.

Henry Seeks an Ally

Abroad, the year 1517 turned out much as Wolsey had foreseen. Maximilian's betrayal of Henry's trust at Brussels in January did not lead to disaster for England, for eight months later Charles of the Netherlands, now king of Castile, informed Francis I that he could not carry out the terms they had signed at Noyon. His new subjects in Castile would never permit the return of Navarre to France, nor could he afford to wait years for the infant French princess, Charlotte, to become old enough for him to marry. Yet Francis dared not attempt to enforce the treaty by arms. An apoplectic stroke had recently made it clear that Maximilian's death could not be far ahead, and that the election of a new emperor would soon dominate European diplomacy. Ambitious Francis planned to win the Imperial crown for himself, but he knew that Charles of Castile, Maximilian's grandson and heir, would be a powerful rival candidate. If the electors chose Francis, he would obviously require all the friends he could muster to support his imperial authority; and if they chose Charles, Francis would still need allies to relax the stranglehold which Charles's dominions, old and new, would exert against most of his eastern, south-eastern, and south-western frontiers. Above everything, Francis knew he must be ready for Maximilian's death, and neither distracted nor weakened by other affairs. Similarly, Charles wanted peace, and, ironically, before the close of the year, both he and Francis were seeking an understanding with Henry. The year, which had begun with Henry's isolation in Europe, ended with him being flattered and cajoled by the very powers who had ignored him. Charles approached him through his aunt, Queen Catherine; Francis pointedly refused further support to Albany in Scotland; and, early in 1518, Leo X completed the diplomatic wooing by sending Cardinal Campeggio to invite Henry to join a crusade against the Turks.

With Wolsey's help, Henry took this change of fortune very calmly. He refused Campeggio permission to cross from Calais to Dover until his ministers had examined his papers, and declared themselves assured that none of his instructions threatened the independence of the crown. Significantly, the ministers only announced themselves satisfied after Campeggio had received from Rome the letters necessary to appoint Wolsey *legatus a latere*, and to remove from the see of Bath and Wells Adrian de Castello, one of Wolsey's opponents. At length, in July 1518, Campeggio and his party, richly adorned with clothing and equipment lent by Wolsey, made an impressive progress from Dover through London to Greenwich. Henry received Campeggio and Wolsey as legates, 'as though bothe had come from Rome'. Towards the end of the summer the admiral of France and the bishop of Paris arrived to negotiate an Anglo-French treaty, and early in October they reached agreement with Wolsey. In exchange for the return of Tournai, always troublesome and expensive for England to hold, Henry agreed to receive 600,000 crowns in twelve annual instalments, and, for the loss of the bishopric, Wolsey extracted an annual pension of 12,000 livres. A marriage alliance between the dauphin, a babe in arms, and the two-year-old Princess Mary marked the opening of this new era of Anglo-French understanding. Moreover, Henry and Francis decided to join with Leo X and invite Maximilian, Charles of Castile, and the heads of all other states in western and central Europe to resolve to live in peace among themselves, and to join together to repel the dangerous incursions of the heathen Turks. English diplomacy appeared to be moulding a new Europe: all eyes seemed to be turned on London—and the king. Naturally, Henry and Wolsey had to arrange ceremonies, banquets, and entertainments magnificent enough to mark and match their diplomatic achievements, and to impress the many high-ranking visitors in the capital. Both of them delighted in such pleasant tasks.

The celebrations to mark the treaty with France began in St. Paul's on Sunday, 3 October. In the presence of Henry, but not of Catherine, who stayed at Greenwich because she was again advanced in pregnancy, Wolsey said Mass, and the representatives of the signatories to the treaty publicly acknowledged their undertakings. Richard Pace delivered 'a good and sufficiently long oration' in elegant Latin. He sang the praises of the two cardinal-legates, but above all he paid high tribute to Henry, who sat below him in a seat covered with cloth of gold. Without any sense of inappropriateness to the occasion, Pace spoke of him as a gifted leader in war. His achievements remained un-dimmed even when compared with those of other outstanding soldier-kings. From St. Paul's the distinguished company filed to the palace of the bishop of London for dinner, and in the evening met again at York House, Wolsey's palace in Whitehall, to enjoy a banquet and entertainment in the large, lavishly decorated hall. The supreme moment of this never-to-be-forgotten evening was reached when Henry and his sister Mary led ten other masked dancers, uniformly dressed in green satin overlaid with cloth of gold, through a series of energetic figures. Two days later, the same company of ambassadors, nobles, and diplomats assembled at Greenwich for the betrothal of Princess Mary and Dauphin Francis. It was another solemn and richly dressed occasion. Flanked on one side by the two cardinals and on the other by his wife, his daughter, and his sister, Henry listened while Cuthbert Tunstal, one of his ministers, opened the formalities with a Latin oration. In splendid periods, which were fully appreciated by the scholars present, Tunstal tritely hailed this indissoluble marriage as symbol and guarantee of the perpetual peace newly signed between England and France. He paid compliments to Mary's beauty, and tactfully drew attention to her love for Henry—'see how she jumps forward from her nurse's lap when she catches sight of her father'. Admiral Bonnivet stood proxy for the infant bridegroom, Wolsey put a diamond ring on Mary's tiny finger, and the ceremony ended with the two cardinals saying Mass. Feasting, gambling, and entertainment filled the next two days, and all ended with a final reception given by Charles and Mary Brandon. The French ambassadors took back to France a party of Englishmen, who had instructions to hand over Tournai to Francis, and at the English court they left behind four hostages as a pledge that they would fulfil their part of the financial agreement.

Within four short months this mirage of perpetual peace in Europe faded away. Maximilian died in January 1519, and overnight the seven German princes whose votes would elect the new emperor became the most important men in Europe. The electors had two motives—to squeeze all the personal profit they could from the election, and to choose the emperor best suited to the interests of themselves and other German princes. Both Francis I and Charles of Castile, the only two serious candidates, spent large and welcome sums of money trying to persuade individual electors to vote for them. Yet the electors did not think that either candidate would make their ideal emperor. Francis was not a German; and the addition of the Empire to Charles's expansive dominions elsewhere could easily mean that he would use his immense wealth and power to limit the independence of the princes, and demand German men and money to fight wars from which the electors could expect no gain.

Puckishly, Maximilian had once suggested that Henry should become the next emperor. Henry did not seem to take this suggestion too seriously, but he never quite dismissed it from his mind. In May 1519 he sent Richard Pace to Germany, empty-handed but heavily loaded with vague and confused instructions. If he had any opportunity to do so, Pace was to explain how suitable and dignified an emperor Henry would make, and, if his arguments seemed to be making an impression on any of the electors, he had authority to strengthen them by promising to give the electors money once the elections had been satisfactorily settled. But Pace was bidden to use discretion in such advocacy, and avoid alienating either of the two main candidates. He should allow the electors who preferred Francis to gain the impression that Henry was on their side, and Charles's supporters that Henry agreed with them. But Henry made it clear to Pace himself that the worst result would be for the electors to choose Francis. Charles never made Henry jealous as Francis did, and most Englishmen found it more natural to despise the jaunty French than to quarrel with the Netherlanders. In May 1519, at the insistence of his councillors, Henry agreed to dismiss from court Nicholas Carew and three other young lords-in-waiting who had shared and encouraged his life of pleasure. They had lately visited the court of Francis I, and had returned 'all Frenche in eatyng, drynkyng, and apparell, yea, and in French vices and bragges', so that they openly scorned the lack of style and old-fashioned routine of the English court. Their places were taken by four older and more sober knights, who did not irritatingly make supercilious comparisons at every opportunity, but who found themselves constantly breathless and exhausted with the dancing, masking, and hunting, which Henry required of them.

Pace carried through his delicate mission with skill. From the elector-archbishop of Trier came the first encouraging words that he might seriously consider voting for Henry, and when, later, the archbishop of Mainz, another elector, suggested that if Henry would only bribe the electors as Francis and Charles were doing he would stand a chance of success, Pace hurried to the Hanse merchants to raise a loan. But he steadfastly refused to give away the king's money until after the election. Pace's reports caused Henry for a few days to become excited with the possibility of being chosen emperor, but no elector ever gave him solid support, and Pace was wise not to throw money into a hopeless cause. At Frankfurt on 28 June, the electors declared Charles of Castile the victor. Pace had been so circumspect in his diplomacy that Charles's representatives at Frankfurt wrote to Spain that English intervention had been helpful in their cause; and for his part, Francis seemed happy enough to accept Henry's assurance that he had supported the French candidature as long as it had stood a chance of success. Henry was pleased with Pace's work. When he learned of the sums Charles had spent on being elected, he shuddered to think how easily he too could have lost a fortune.

One of the clauses of the Anglo-French treaty signed in London in October 1518 had stated that Henry and Francis should hold a conference in the near future. The Imperial election delayed the plans, but eventually the two kings agreed to meet near Guînes in the Pas de Calais during the summer of 1520. Both left it to Wolsey to make all necessary arrangements. But Henry also wished to confer with the new emperor, for he was anxious that Charles should not misunderstand the purpose of his meeting with Francis. So while some of Wolsey's men were arranging for an army of English craftsmen and labourers to cross the Channel to prepare the site at Balinghem near Guînes, and while others were buying rich hangings and clothing, and earmarking adequate supplies of food and drink for the great occasion, Wolsey himself was negotiating with the court of Emperor Charles V, to arrange a meeting which would undo, or at least neutralise, all that was to be achieved so expensively and flamboyantly at Guînes. Henry's official aim was to reduce the tension between France and the Empire, to promote peace in Christendom, and to unite Christian monarchs in a crusade against the Infidel. But few took such ideal motives at their face value. It seemed clear to most observers that war between France and the Empire could not be long postponed. Francis and Charles both hoped to win Henry's favourable neutrality, if not his support: for their part Henry and Wolsey were seeking their own best interests. Already they were inclined to think they would be better served by an Anglo-Imperial understanding.

Wolsey experienced some difficulty in timing events during that eventful summer of 1520. Francis insisted that his meeting with Henry should not be later than the end of May, because the pregnant Queen Claude would not be able to attend much later than that. On the other hand, Charles preferred his meeting to be in June, and yet Henry thought it better to see Charles before he met Francis. In the end the time-table degenerated into a scramble. Henry, Catherine, and the main body of courtiers left Greenwich for France on 21 May. They arrived at Canterbury on the 25th, and received the somewhat un-expected news that Charles's ships were lying off Dover. Henry, there-fore, postponed his date of sailing, met Charles at Dover, and for the next four days conferred with him at Canterbury. On the last day of the month Charles embarked at Sandwich to return to the Netherlands, and Henry at Dover to cross to Calais. Four days had allowed little time for extravagant entertainment or elaborate ceremony, but the two monarchs had achieved some serious discussion.

By contrast the Balinghem meeting at the Field of the Cloth of Gold had pomp, revelry, and feasting but no real significance. Henry sailed

in *Henry Grâce à Dieu*, and on 4 June set out from Calais. Around the
vast, temporary, but lavishly equipped and decorated palace built for
Henry and Catherine, Wolsey's men had pitched nearly 3000 tents, gay
with heraldic devices, for the housing of the king's ministers, nobles,
and soldiers. Every nobleman, himself richly dressed, brought with him
as full a company of liveried retainers as he could muster, if not
necessarily afford. Wolsey chose crimson velvet for his large body-
guard and crimson silk for himself, and when the two kings met alone
in 'the royall rich tent, all of clothe of gold . . . within hanged of the
richest Arras, newly contrived and made', Henry wore 'a garment of
Cloth of Silver, of Damaske, ribbed wyth Clothe of Gold so thicke
as might bee', and Francis 'clothe of silver, culpond with clothe of
golde, of damaske cantell wise . . . and over that a cloke of broched
satten, with gold of purple coloure, wrapped about his body traverse,
beded from the shulder to the waste, fastened in the lope of the first
fold'. Both kings took stock of each other. Afterwards, Henry admitted
that Francis had a good figure and a cheerful countenance, and Francis
admired Henry's upstanding body, albeit *un peu grasset*, his gold-red
beard, and his rich display. The jousting, feasting, and entertainment
were all superb; manners and ceremonial were perfect except for a
moment of truth when, in what should have been a friendly wrestle,
Francis threw Henry, and an enraged king picked himself up vowing
revenge. During the last night workmen transformed part of the tilting
yard into a chapel, and the next morning, 23 June, Wolsey assisted by
several bishops sang Mass in the presence of four French cardinals and
the two courts. Hardly one item in the whole of the long meeting
could have been made more dramatic or impressive, yet out of it all
came nothing lasting. True, Henry and Wolsey congratulated themselves on taking away the breath of the French, and leaving them
speculating how so moderately prosperous a country as England could
possibly afford such lavish expenditure, but the only political result of
the meeting was that Henry became convinced that war between
Francis and Charles was imminent. The engagement of Princess Mary
and the dauphin still stood as the symbol of the Anglo-French alliance,
but it did not seem likely that Henry would be fighting in support of
Francis when war began.

From the Field of the Cloth of Gold, Henry returned to Calais, and
a fortnight later rode out to Gravelines to renew his conference with the

emperor. For three or four days the two monarchs and the two courts
lived together first at Gravelines and then at Calais. The entertainment
was royal enough, but never approached the extravagances of
Balinghem. Both sides considered business more important than display. When the conference ended, Henry hoped that he had left
Charles under the impression that he would be on his side in the
coming struggle, and that he had no intention of allowing Princess
Mary to marry the dauphin; for his part Charles trusted that Henry
would be so dazzled by the proposal that Mary one day should become
empress, that he would remain pro-Imperial or, at least, anti-French.

Buckingham and Luther Condemned

Within a few days, Henry took his court back to England. He had
given two precious summer months to diplomacy, and he compensated himself by hunting relentlessly from daybreak to sundown during
the rest of the year. 'He spares no pains to convert the sport of hunting
into a martyrdom', observed a contemporary. It was almost as if he
were working off on his horses and the hunted stags and boars the
resentment and frustration he had had to keep bottled up during his
days on the Continent. Or it may have been that in excessive hunting
and in such endless jousting, feasting, and entertainment as took place
at Greenwich during Christmastide 1520, Henry was trying to forget
the personal worry which increasingly thrust itself into his mind. For
the last two years, despite all possible medical advice, Catherine had
failed to conceive. She was now 35 years of age. Every month made it
more unlikely that she would ever bear Henry a son. Already men
were speculating upon who would succeed Henry to the throne, and
on no other topic was the king so sensitive as this. He tried but failed
to push the problem from his mind; he feared that the Tudor dynasty
would end with him, and end perhaps in civil war, if he and Catherine
did not have a son. Mary could carry the throne either to her future
husband—or a more remote possibility—to her son, but no son-in-law
or even grandson, whether he were foreign king or English nobleman,
would be a successor wholly acceptable to Henry, or, he thought, to
his subjects. Nor was the recognition of Henry Fitzroy a satisfactory
substitute for a son born in wedlock, although later, in 1526, in desperation and anger over the failure of negotiations for Mary's marriage,

14 THE DEPARTURE OF HENRY FROM DOVER FOR THE FIELD OF THE CLOTH OF GOLD
Detail from the contemporary painting at Hampton Court; reproduced by gracious permission of H.M. The Queen

15 HENRY AT THE FIELD OF THE CLOTH OF GOLD

Detail from the contemporary painting at Hampton Court; reproduced by gracious permission of H.M. The Queen

Henry conferred upon the boy the titles of duke of Richmond, duke of Somerset, and lord high admiral of England, and even toyed with the idea of marrying him to Mary, his half-sister.

In such circumstances it behoved anyone who had the slightest chance of ever succeeding to the throne to be most circumspect. The easy way in which the king had contrived to have de la Pole condemned to death in 1513 shouted warning. But the duke of Buckingham, a direct descendant from Thomas of Woodstock, youngest son of Edward III, blundered on heedless of danger. He despised Wolsey, openly showed disdain for his lowly birth, and spoke out against what he mistakenly thought was his pro-French policy. That was dangerous enough, but soon afterwards he allowed Wolsey to hear that he had been speculating upon the chances of himself or his son succeeding to the throne. It was not difficult for Wolsey to find some of Buckingham's disgruntled servants—his chancellor, his confessor, and a discharged surveyor—to give evidence that Buckingham had been wishing (or plotting?) to hasten the king's death so that he could gain the throne, and so fulfil the prophecy of the Carthusian monk, whom he had consulted some years previously, *that he should have all*. In Henry's highly suspicious, almost frightened, mind, such flimsy evidence bespoke treason. He summoned Buckingham to London, imprisoned him in the Tower, and in May 1521 brought the formal charge against him. The verdict was never in doubt: not one of the score of nobles who heard the case, Norfolk, Suffolk, Dorset, and the rest, dared defy Henry's wishes. Nor did Henry, *gracious prince* though Buckingham called him, show more mercy than to replace the barbarous sentence of hanging, drawing, and quartering, by the more humane one of beheading, and this in spite of the loyalty with which Buckingham had served Henry VII and himself, in spite of Catherine's plea to forgive a nobleman who had always befriended her, and in spite of the shock and disapproval with which the Londoners heard the verdict. For two or three days Henry was too distracted and disturbed in his mind to settle to his usual pleasures, but the loyalty and flattery of his court soon restored his self-confidence. He had little compassion and, in spite of his intelligence, he easily persuaded himself that what he wished to believe was the truth. To him it was soon clear that Buckingham had been plotting to overthrow the Tudors so that the Staffords might succeed to the throne. His peers had condemned him in open trial.

There could hardly have been any other just or wise outcome of his wickedness but immediate execution.

In the very month that Buckingham died on the scaffold, Henry completed the writing of his book, *Assertion of the Seven Sacraments.* Ever since Luther had published his *Ninety-five Theses* in 1517, Henry, encouraged by Wolsey, had been desultorily preparing a reply. In April 1521, Pace found him reading and 'dispraising' Luther's new book, *Babylonian Captivity of the Church*, and this study seems to have provoked enough indignation to blow the embers of his original purpose into fire and enable him to finish his neglected task. Automatically as a prince, he condemned all rebellion against established authority, but he attacked Luther as much for his theology as for the political consequences of his heresy. Henry liked to count himself among the humanists and usually considered himself a moderate reformer like More and Erasmus, but in his enthusiasm to demonstrate that 'by one man's disobedience many were made sinners', he went to the other extreme and expressed unshakeable loyalty to the papacy. He submitted the early drafts of his work to More and other scholars for criticism and amendment. He accepted their suggestions for improving his Latin style, and for a more logical order in his arguments—More later explained that he was 'a sorter-out and placer' of the principal matters in the book—but when More gently and diplomatically pointed out that he might one day have cause to declare war on the pope in his capacity as an Italian prince and consequently that it might be wise to touch upon the papal authority 'more slenderly', Henry brushed aside his cautious advice. Nothing was too strong to say in favour of Rome. Later that summer, John Clerk, bishop of Bath and Wells and ambassador to Rome, presented the pope with two copies of Henry's book, elegantly bound in sheepskin and cloth of gold. Leo warmly welcomed Henry's gift and the flattering words with which Clerk presented it. In return, in October 1521, he granted Henry's request to bestow on him the title *Fidei Defensor.* Two years later his successor, Clement VII, confirmed it. Henry lived to regret much of what he had written in *Assertion of the Seven Sacraments.* He tried to throw the responsibility for his arguments on to the shoulders of his advisers, especially More, but to his new title he clung tenaciously. In 1523 Clement wrote *we approve . . . the title . . . to be your own for ever,* but despite this ambiguous phrasing, twenty years later, the Act of the

King's Style assumed and confirmed that the title was 'united and annexed for ever to be the imperial crown of this his Highness's realm of England'.

Renewed War Against France

In the spring of 1521 French and Spanish forces came to blows in Navarre, and later in the year fighting broke out on the north-east frontier of France. Both King Francis and Emperor Charles claimed to be the injured party, and both appealed to Henry to put into force the Treaty of London and side with him against the aggressor. To discover who was the aggressor, Wolsey, with Henry's approval, called a conference at Calais. It lasted five months, but it was never more than an elaborate pretence, for neither Henry nor Wolsey had ever any intention of allying with Francis. Henry still preferred the drab and serious Charles to the gay and dashing Francis; Wolsey relied upon Charles's support at the next papal election; and both valued possible developments in Anglo-Burgundian trade. Moreover, Leo X opposed Francis, and both Wolsey and Henry still wished to be on the pope's side. Hardly had the Calais conference begun before Wolsey slipped away to Bruges officially to persuade Charles to give his Calais representatives authority to negotiate a truce, but actually to initial a treaty by which Henry and Charles bound themselves as allies, agreed that Charles should marry Mary Tudor when she was 12 years old, and planned a joint invasion of France. The war could not begin at once. Impetuous Henry was enthusiastically hatching plans to defeat the French navy in the Channel, and land an invasion army in France, but even he had to recognise the truth of Pace's dictum that nothing could be done 'till the convention at Calais is concluded, as it would be a manifest derision to treat of peace and send men to make war'. Moreover, he had no money for war. It pleased him that through Wolsey he should be posing as arbiter between the emperor and the king of France, but the practical advantage of the Calais conference was that it was postponing, until 1522 at least, the necessity of finding money to raise troops. Henry's lively court and previous adventures across the Channel had exhausted the treasure left by Henry VII, and in his less exuberant moments Henry VIII realised that it was not going to be easy to draw sufficient taxes from Englishmen, who had no love for France but still less for paying the cost of war.

Wolsey returned to England at the end of November. Already Charles, Leo, and their Italian allies had won a major victory over the French in Lombardy, and Henry was savouring the prospect of joining in the pillaging of France in the following year. But less than a fortnight before Christmas, news reached England that Leo X had died suddenly. Immediately Henry sent off Pace to Rome to press Wolsey's claim to the vacant papal throne. Pace travelled first to Ghent to see the emperor and remind him that he had promised to support Wolsey. Charles dutifully gave him letters for the cardinals, and on 26 December Pace resumed his long journey. But he was far too late arriving in Rome. Florence greeted him with the news that the cardinals had already elected the new pope—Adrian VI. Even Wolsey's personal letter, which he had sent direct to Cardinal Campeggio, had arrived after the election. But distance and time had not defeated Wolsey. Those who spoke in Rome on the emperor's behalf had not supported him, and without their voices, his own strong, alien personality could never have won sufficient votes for success. The conclave had considered his name at an early stage of the election, but had quickly dismissed it. England's consolation was that the cardinals could have chosen a worse pope, for Adrian, a Netherlander and an old tutor of Charles V, looked very likely to maintain the alliance against France.

Henry declared war on Francis in May 1522. Two months previously he had already announced that he was ready to defend the Low Countries during the emperor's absence in Spain, and Francis had counter-attacked by seizing English ships trading with Bordeaux and by seeking another military understanding with the Scots. In June Charles arrived in England on his way to Spain. Henry spared no pains to entertain him in the grand style as befitted not only the head of the Holy Roman Empire, but also his dear kinsman, future son-in-law, and devoted ally. At Dover, Henry proudly showed his guest over *Henry Grâce à Dieu* and other warships anchored in the harbour; at Greenwich, Charles spoke with his aunt, Queen Catherine, and for the first time met his affianced wife, the seven-year-old Mary. From Greenwich Henry and Charles rode to Southwark and London, thence to Richmond and Hampton Court, thence to Windsor to confer, thence to Winchester, and finally to Southampton, where Charles rejoined his fleet of 200 ships. Everywhere excited, gazing crowds admired and cheered the two monarchs. London marked their visit with elaborate pageants, music, processions, and extravagant compliments, and whenever he could, Henry took Charles hunting or amused him with tourneys. Hall summed it up—'nothyng lacked that might be gotten, to chere the Emperor and his Lordes, and al that came in his compaignie, were highly feasted'. The Windsor treaty, strengthened with solemn oaths taken in St. George's Chapel, bound the two sovereigns into permanent alliance and friendship, denounced France, made detailed arrangements for the eventual marriage of Mary and Charles, and even agreed that if Henry had no son to succeed him, the eldest male child born to Mary and Charles should be the next king of England.

That year, 1522, Henry limited his war effort to a series of sporadic attacks. Surrey led them—in July, in the area of Cherbourg and along the Breton coast, and in September, in Artois—but they were too inadequately supplied and organised to be anything more effective than nuisance raids. From his estates, fines, and customs duties Henry could confidently budget for his court expenses and the payment of his administrators and representatives both at home and abroad. But war, as ever, destroyed all sane accounting. In 1522 Wolsey tried to meet the war bill by 'voluntary' loans. London gave £20,000 immediately, and during the summer and autumn the rest of England paid into the treasury a further £350,000. Even these large sums fell far short of war expenses, and it became obvious that if war were to continue in 1523—and both Henry and Wolsey were determined to fulfil their agreement with Charles—Wolsey must face the disagreeable necessity of calling parliament.

In April 1523 Henry opened the sessions, and entrusted Cuthbert Tunstal, the newly appointed bishop of London, with the task of explaining why it was necessary for parliament to meet. In a long, erudite speech in English, but interspersed with numerous Latin quotations and tags, Tunstal praised Henry as an ideal king of great judgment, learning, experience and diligence. Not only must subjects obey him, but they must be co-operative among themselves, for it was a token of 'a malicious mind when one person of a realm destroyeth or hurteth another'. Part of the king's duty was to protect his people against hostile powers, 'and the whole realm is bound to aid the king in this cause to the uttermost of their power, and especially lords and knights which be as the hands of the politic body, and other inferior

men of war that be the small fingers of these hands'. The commons
retired, and elected Sir Thomas More as their speaker. Henry and
Wolsey felt they could rely upon More's loyalty and negotiating skill,
although they knew that More did not share Wolsey's apparent trust
in the emperor's word, nor Henry's naïve belief that the French would
welcome his invading soldiers as liberators from the tyranny of Francis
I. But once the commons began to discuss taxation, it quickly became
clear that the house believed that war would bring England nothing
but heavy expense and unnecessary suffering. Most members had no
objection to raiding French harbours and pillaging French ships, but
they recoiled from the prospect of spending English gold in the
emperor's cause, and becoming engulfed in a long war with France
and Scotland. Wolsey attempted to browbeat and badger them.
'Masters, you have many wise and learned men among you, and sith
I am from the King's own person sent hither unto you for the preserva-
tion of yourselves and all the realm, I think it meet you give me some
reasonable answer.' But all he achieved was what he himself described
as 'a marvellous obstinate silence', for the members refused to answer
except through Mr. Speaker, their 'common mouth'.

Later the commons offered £400,000 instead of the £800,000
demanded by Wolsey. By careful cajoling More managed to raise
this to £600,000 to be spread over a number of years. Wolsey accepted,
but as soon as parliament had been dissolved, he ignored the stipulation
that the grant should be paid by instalments, and instructed the royal
commissioners to collect it all at once. Even so the cash did not reach
the treasury rapidly enough, and Henry's contribution to what was
planned as a triple attack on France was limited to Suffolk leading an
army of 20,000 from Calais across the Somme. Suffolk turned back 40
miles short of Paris. He had found none of the expected support either
from Charles V in the south or from the disaffected duke of Bourbon
in the east, and his own army had achieved nothing but wanton destruction. Against Suffolk's wish Henry had given orders to encourage the
troops to plunder and pillage—'if they should also forbear the profit
of the spoil (the bare hope whereof, though they get little, was great
encouraging to them) they shall have evil will to march far forward,
and their captains shall have much ado to keep them from crying,
"Home! Home"!' Before the end of 1523 it appeared to many, if not
to Henry, that Wolsey's pro-Imperial policy was bankrupt. Not only

had it wasted money and antagonised London and the commons, but it had also endangered northern England. Only Lord Dacres's military and diplomatic skill west of the Pennines, and the baseless Scottish dread of a second Flodden had saved the northern counties from serious punitive raids, for not until the summer of 1523 had Henry either time or forces to devote to defending the border. Wolsey himself was bitterly disappointed, for England's campaign against France had not induced Charles to support his claim in Rome when Adrian VI died in September. Once again Charles had written letters on his behalf, but through his representatives in the Vatican had secured the election of Giulio de' Medici, who took the title of Clement VII.

After so disastrous a year, it is little wonder that no English army invaded France in 1524. Henry had neither money nor heart for it, and when towards the end of the year Clement signed a treaty with France and Venice against the emperor, Henry faced the unpleasant option of either coming to terms with Francis or risking diplomatic isolation. He invited a French envoy, nicknamed John Joachim, to stay in London, but fortunately had done no more than this officially before he received the startling news of Charles's unexpected victory and the capture of Francis himself at Pavia in Lombardy in February 1525. Immediately Henry forgot the broken promises and frustrations of the previous two years, and began to dream again of conquering part of France. He told the astonished courier that he was as welcome to him as Gabriel had been to the Virgin Mary, and he ordered bonfires to be lit, and wine to be given to the London citizens. In St. Paul's the court and diplomatic corps heard Mass and listened to the choir singing a joyful *Te Deum*. Queen Catherine could not have imagined better news, for she had no wish to see the alliance between her husband and nephew broken, and Henry's own joy was greater still when he learned that Richard de la Pole, Edmund's younger brother and the last of the family, lay among the dead on the field of Pavia. Bishop Tunstal and Sir Richard Wingfield were soon on their way to Spain with serious proposals that Charles should depose the Valois house from the French throne, and, by joint invasion with Henry, should enable the Empire and England to satisfy their 'just claims' in France. But when after seven weeks of hazardous sailing and horse-riding Tunstal and Wingfield came to Toledo, they found not a jubilant Charles, but a Charles full of complaint that Henry had not helped him since 1523, that he had stood

idly by in 1524 while Imperial troops were invading Provence and
besieging Marseilles, that he had lately been attempting to make a
separate peace with France, and that Wolsey had called him a faithless
liar and had insulted his ambassador. He accepted the emerald ring
which Tunstal had brought from Princess Mary, but soon made it clear
that he no more intended marrying Mary than invading France. Like
Henry he was acutely short of money. Payment to his Italian troops
was badly in arrears, and he was grievously disturbed by the news of
the Turkish advance up the Danube and of the Peasants' Revolt in
Germany.

Charles's lack of enthusiasm for war against France might have been
expected to dash Henry's fondest hopes, but when news of it arrived in
London, it was not unwelcome. Later dispatches to Toledo show that
once his initial excitement had burned itself out, Henry had realised
he must have peace. Despite Pavia, he considered the future of Europe
to be uncertain enough to require him to be free from all political
entanglements, and, more ominous still, the royal commissioners were
encountering considerable resistance in gathering taxes. To finance
renewed war Wolsey had attempted to levy a new tax, which with unconscious irony he christened the Amicable Grant. The official bonfires
which celebrated Pavia and the government argument which called for
immediate action to exploit the favourable position in France roused
more opposition than enthusiasm, for many believed that for private
gain and ambition Wolsey had talked an unwilling Henry into fighting
the war. In East Anglia and Kent men openly refused to pay, and Wolsey
himself, as commissioner for London, met with no more success than
did the noblemen whom he had appointed commissioners elsewhere.
In desperate anxiety to justify his policy in Henry's eyes, Wolsey
demanded a sixth of all property and income from those who owned
estates worth more than £50 a year, and a twentieth from estates of
less than £20. Laymen and clergy alike were appalled at the weight of
the tax. They rejected the basis of its assessment, and the unconsti-
tutional method of levying it. They loathed Wolsey's arrogance,
efficiency, and power, and resented his fabulous and increasing personal
wealth in such difficult times. Only Henry's statesmanlike intervention
saved an ugly situation. He denied all knowledge of Wolsey's assess-
ments: he only wished to receive, he said, such money as his subjects
would freely give him. He summoned the great council to enquire

why Wolsey had demanded 'a sixth of every man's substance', and issued a royal pardon to all who had been arrested for refusing to pay. Wolsey sought to save his face by protesting that he had only obeyed the will of the council. He denied that he, personally, had ever wished for so stringent a demand, and asserted that he had pleaded the people's cause with the king. These justifications deceived very few. The courage of the city and the gentry in refusing to pay had increased popular hatred of the cardinal. Wolsey, wrote Skelton, robs the king and feathers his own nest,

> *And useth such abusion*
> *That in the conclusion*
> *All cometh to confusion.*
> *He is so ambitious*
> *So shameless, and so vicious,*
> *And so superstitious*
> *And so much oblivious*
> *From whence that he came. . . .*

Though Tunstal was still negotiating at Toledo, Henry agreed that Wolsey should approach Louise of Savoy, the regent of France during the imprisonment of Francis, and try and make peace. By the end of August 1525 English and French representatives sealed the new treaty at The Moor, one of Wolsey's houses, and shattered Henry's dream that one day his grandchild might succeed to both the English and the Imperial thrones. In September Henry formally freed Charles from his engagement to Mary, announced that he had no objection to his betrothal and marriage to Isabella of Portugal, but required that out of Isabella's dowry Charles should repay the loans he had had from England. In the following January, Francis I regained his freedom on exacting terms which he never intended to honour, but despite patient work by Tunstal and other ministers, Henry never recovered a penny of the 500,000 crowns which he claimed Charles had borrowed from him. His much-prized and vaunted friendship with the emperor had emptied his treasury, soured his relations with his subjects to the point of threatened rebellion and widespread whispering of treasonable words, and ended in a treaty with their mutual enemy. In May 1526 the diplomatic wheel came full circle when Francis, Clement VII, Venice, Florence and Milan, under nothing less than the protection of Henry Tudor, signed the alliance known as the League of Cognac.

These were dark days for Queen Catherine. In Henry's friendship
with her nephew, Charles, she had found considerable compensation
for her chronic ill-health and her inability to satisfy Henry's desire for
a son. Now that her husband was the ally of her nephew's enemies,
she worried what was likely to happen to Mary, beloved by both her
and Henry and the one strong bond between them. Already she and
Mary had been separated, for Henry had ordered his daughter to
Ludlow to take up her duties as princess of Wales. To add to Catherine's
gloom Henry had dismissed some of her favourite ladies-in-waiting,
and had titled Bessie Blount's son as if he were heir to the throne.
Most cruel blow of all, his brief, formal visits to her apartments made
it abundantly clear that he sought and preferred the company and
affection of other ladies.

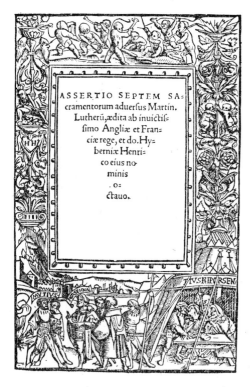

Title-page of Henry's attack on Luther, 1521

3 THE INADEQUACY OF WOLSEY

The third day comes a frost, a killing frost;
And, when he thinks, good easy man, full surely
His greatness is a-ripening, nips his root,
And then he falls, as I do.

SHAKESPEARE

HENRY had been thinking of putting Catherine aside some months before he first met Anne Boleyn. Long ago she had ceased to be his chief confidante and prop, and for the last ten years he had shown her less and less affection. He still insisted that she received every courtesy as queen and with conscious consideration he kept his mistresses in the background of court life. Could Catherine have brought herself to flatter and cajole, she might have longer resisted the challenge of younger and more lively women. For Henry, however, bluntness and independence of mind did little to redeem her lined face and dumpy figure. Nevertheless, though she had ceased to attract him physically, she inspired him with a curious respect. He was half afraid of her, and was certainly apprehensive of displeasing her. If she had given him a son to succeed him, he would still have enjoyed his mistresses, but would never have considered finding another wife. But he could not understand why God had denied him a male heir. Catherine had been pregnant at least six times, but on all but one occasion the pregnancy had ended either in miscarriage, still-birth, or the almost immediate death of the child. Only Mary lived. Yet both he and Catherine had always been diligent in their religious duties: the church had never had royal children more loyal. Pure logic therefore drove Henry to assume that denying a son was God's way of showing His displeasure, and the only possible cause of that displeasure was that Catherine had once been

57

Arthur's wife. The commandment in *Leviticus* was clear enough—
'Thou shalt not uncover the nakedness of thy brother's wife'. And two
chapters further on the law prescribed the penalty—'. . . they shall be
childless'. Significantly this particular punishment was reserved ex-
clusively for those who defied the ban on marrying a brother's widow.
It was true that a text in *Deuteronomy* bade a man take to wife the childless widow of his brother, but the Church had always upheld the
Leviticus injunction, and, apparently, not even the papal dispensation
had persuaded God to withhold the penalty from Henry. Until the
wrong had been put right, until he, a bachelor in the eyes of God, had
ceased to live incestuously with his brother's wife, he believed he could
not again expect to find favour with God. Henry Fitzroy proved he
could beget sons of other women. God's denial applied to Catherine
only.

During his years of optimism and pride in Catherine, Henry had
encountered no difficulty in suppressing his doubt on the validity of his
marriage, but from 1525 onwards, circumstances combined to encourage its rapid growth in his mind. Catherine blamed Wolsey for
Henry's increasing coldness towards her. She detested his pro-French
policy which she believed he was thrusting on an unwilling Henry, and
she thought he was making her the scapegoat for her emperor-nephew's
offences. During the whole of 1526 there was no one in London to
represent Charles, for the new ambassador, Don Iñigo de Mendoza, had
been arrested 'in error' on his way through France and had spent most
of the year in a Normandy prison. Not until Henry had fully committed himself to the French alliance and the League of Cognac, did
Francis discover the 'mistake', and free Mendoza with humble apologies.
In February 1527, close on Mendoza's heels, the bishop of Tarbes
arrived in London at the head of a French embassy determined to tie
England still closer to France and to renew the war against the Empire.
Henry and Wolsey treated Mendoza politely but coldly, and Wolsey
did all he could to prevent him from meeting Queen Catherine. By
contrast they received the French ambassadors with banquets and
tournaments both at Greenwich and London, and enthusiastically
began treaty negotiations. Early in the discussions it was said that the
bishop of Tarbes had questioned the validity of Mary's claim to the
English throne because Henry had married his brother's widow, but
on the last day of April this moral scruple did not prevent him from

signing the new Anglo-French treaty, which arranged that Princess Mary, only 11 years old but a much-promised bride, should marry the duke of Orleans, the second son of Francis I.

The Boleyn Family

By the time this treaty had been negotiated, Henry had fallen deeply in love with the dark-haired Anne Boleyn. Five or six years earlier he had taken Anne's sister, Mary, as his mistress, but apparently had never had for her the overpowering longing he now felt for Anne. In the early months of 1527 these two daughters of Sir Thomas and Lady Elizabeth Boleyn were members of Queen Catherine's household. As young girls both had spent some time at the French court, but they had been such unimportant members of that glittering, gay household that it is most difficult to trace their movements in the records. By February 1520, Mary, probably the elder of the two, had returned to England, for in that month she married William Carey. Later in the year she and her husband, as well as Sir Thomas and Lady Boleyn, attended Henry and Catherine at the Field of the Cloth of Gold. Apparently Anne was still at the court of Queen Claude of France. In 1520 Wolsey had considered that she would be a suitable wife for James Butler, son of the Irish earl of Ormond, but his plans had gone astray, and certainly by 1523 he had abandoned them. Meanwhile, Anne had recrossed the Channel and had joined Catherine's household. Almost immediately young Henry Percy, the heir to the earldom of Northumberland, had offered to marry her, but both his father and Wolsey intervened. The earl had already promised that his son would marry Mary Talbot, the earl of Shrewsbury's daughter, and Wolsey was still making plans for Anne to make the diplomatic marriage with Butler. They sent Percy north to become deputy-warden of the Marches, and a year or so later he married Mary Talbot. Anne also withdrew from court.

During the next three or four years Henry heaped honours on Sir Thomas Boleyn. In April 1522 he made him treasurer of the royal household. In 1523 and 1524 he appointed him to several lucrative offices in Kent, Essex, and Nottinghamshire, and in the following year raised him to the rank of viscount. These benefactions rewarded faithful and useful service to the crown, but they were probably partly inspired by Mary, for *Mistress Carey* was at the height of her influence during these years. In 1526 she gave birth to a son, inevitably christened *Henry*, and destined to become Lord Hunsdon, a favoured cousin of Queen Elizabeth. Court gossip whispered that the child's father was someone more important than William Carey, but court gossip is not always a reliable source of information.

Unobtrusively, Anne returned to court some time in 1526. We do not know the date of her birth, but at that time she was probably about 20 years old. Outwardly she had little to distinguish her from the other young ladies who attended the queen. She was fairly tall, with attractive dark eyes and long black hair. Like most of her companions she danced well, but she seems to have had more than ordinary talent for music. This interest, common to them both, may have first drawn Henry's attention towards her, but not even the collection of Henry's love-letters, which have fortunately survived, tells us definitely either when or why she first attracted him. What is quite clear, however, is that Anne kept Henry's advances at arm's length. She had no wish to become Henry's mistress. Bessie Blount had given the king a son, but she was now married off to an obscure knight. Her own sister, the friendly and easy-going Mary, had not received rewards which would have satisfied Anne. A brief period of notoriety held no attractions for her. But since Henry did not hide his disquiet about the legality of his marriage to Catherine, Anne early resolved that if ever she gave herself to Henry, it would be not as his mistress, but as his new queen.

To play for such high stakes with any hope of winning called for self-confidence, steady nerves, and subtlety. Anne had all three. Henry delighted in her company, and when she retired to her father's house at Hever in Kent, his want of her grew into a passion. His early love letters (unfortunately none are dated) voiced the common grievance of lovers that 'already the tedium of absence is too great', and declared that he could not bear to think of being parted from her much longer had he not strong hope of her unchangeable affection for him. Anne continued to stay at Hever, and in a later letter, written in French as were most of his letters to Anne, Henry rebuked her and half-threatened to finish with her if she did not show more co-operation—'. . . if I were certain that you yourself wished this prolonged absence, I could do no other than lament my bad luck and gradually forget my great folly'. Since none of Anne's letters have survived, we can only surmise how she replied to Henry, but clearly she successfully increased his desire for her. A little later he wrote, 'I have endured great agony debating with myself the content of your letters, not knowing how to interpret them, whether to my disadvantage as demonstrated in one place or to my advantage as in another. I implore you let me know plainly your feelings concerning the love that is between us.' In the same letter he asked her outright to be his mistress: '. . . but if you would be a true loyal mistress and friend and give yourself body and heart to me, who have been and will be your most loyal servant (if your hardness does not forbid it), I promise you not only that the name will be yours by right, but also that I shall take you alone for my mistress, cast all others out of my thoughts and affections, and serve you only'. Doubtless Henry considered this a handsome offer, but it did not tempt Anne. Nevertheless, she must have encouraged him in other ways, for out of his next letter shone the joy and happiness which he derived from her reply. He would not be content, he wrote, merely to match the devotion she had expressed, but would always offer her more than she offered him: '. . . henceforward my heart shall be yours alone, would that my body could be yours too, as God can bring about if he so wishes'.

Henry Broaches His Great Matter

For all his brusqueness Henry rarely took quick decisions. He either accepted those of others, first Catherine and then Wolsey, or else he waited until circumstances or flattering friends persuaded him that the right course to follow was the one that coincided with his dearest wishes. This self-deception was sincere and total. For months before he wished to marry Anne Boleyn, he had wrestled with the problem of the lack of a son but had come to no decision. Now his unfulfilled desire for Anne moved him to take action. Early in 1527 he asked several of his more intimate counsellors what they thought about the legality of his marriage. All answered cautiously and indecisively, although some, eager to please, were encouraging, and others, like More, protested that in their judgment they were not 'meet counsellors for your Grace herein'. On 17 May 1527, as a result of his own insistence, Henry appeared in person at Westminster before Wolsey, as cardinal-legate, and Warham, as archbishop of Canterbury, on a charge of having lived incestuously for eighteen years with his brother's widow. Before this ecclesiastical tribunal Henry pretended to defend himself, but from the third meeting of the court on 31 May, Dr. John Bell presented his case. Dr. Richard Wolman led the prosecution. Neither counsel was in a happy position, for though Henry did not want his defence to succeed, he was touchy enough to be most offended if the prosecution pressed its arguments too far.

Wolsey and Warham declined to decide so weighty a matter on their own. They were acutely aware that both at home and abroad Catherine would have powerful sympathisers, and they wished to minimise hostility and opposition by seeking other opinions, and making it appear as if the sheer weight of legal and ecclesiastical argument and authority forced them to take a most unpalatable decision. For this reason they canvassed the bishops, but the bishops disappointed them by not answering with one voice. Too many echoed the opinion of John Fisher of Rochester that since the pope had granted a dispensation, the validity of the royal marriage could hardly be in question. Worse still, the shocking news reached London that on 6 May Imperial troops had sacked Rome and imprisoned the pope in the castle of St. Angelo. By so doing they had transformed the political situation, for now Henry did not face the easy prospect of approaching a fellow member of the League of Cognac for a formal document upholding a decision taken in London, but the forbidding task of trying to persuade a prisoner of his enemy, Charles V, to condemn the emperor's aunt as an adulteress and her only surviving child as a bastard. Therefore, within a few days of its inception it was clear that 'the king's great matter' would take far longer to settle than its sponsors had originally thought. However easily years ago Charles Brandon had used the ecclesiastical courts to put aside an unwanted wife, his brother-in-law, Henry Tudor, was obviously going to encounter major difficulties in trying to achieve the same result by the same methods.

A most serious personal difficulty for Henry was to break his news to Catherine. He put off the awkward moment because he was under the illusion that the Westminster court proceedings were being kept secret. But Catherine had had a verbal report within hours of the first meeting. She had informed Mendoza, and he had seen to it that it was soon the most open secret in the taverns and parlours of London, and furthermore that the whispered story was being told from Catherine's point of view. Consequently, Henry did not take Catherine by surprise when eventually on 22 June, he screwed up his courage to the sticking-place and told her of his troubled conscience and of the obvious cause of God's displeasure. He asked her to leave court and choose a place of retirement. Catherine's tears and disbelief destroyed the effects which Henry had expected from this carefully prepared speech. She pulled away the chief support from under his arguments by declaring that Arthur had never been her husband in anything but name. Her only real husband had been Henry. She ignored Henry's request that she should leave court, and he had not the heart or the resolution to order her to go. Instead he retreated frustrated, angry, and, for the moment at least, defeated.

Both Catherine and Henry sought allies. Catherine sent Francisco Felipez to Spain to beg her nephew, Charles, require the pope both to forbid any decision against her, and revoke Wolsey's legatine powers: Henry, who hitherto had not been enthusiastic for Wolsey's pro-French policy, now agreed that the cardinal should go to France to try and make plans for freeing the pope from the emperor's control. Wolsey crossed the Channel early in July, and for the next month negotiated and feasted royally with French ambassadors at Amiens. First, he proposed that such cardinals as were free of the emperor should assemble at Avignon, and exercise papal authority from there so long as Clement remained an Imperial prisoner. Francis supported this proposal, but neither Avignon, with its association with the Great Schism, nor Wolsey, with his Continental reputation for cunning and self-interest, recommended it to the cardinals. Wolsey had to abandon the suggestion, but in August he pledged England to help finance the French general Lautrec in an attempt to relieve Rome.

Meantime, Henry could not wait for Wolsey's diplomatic plans to mature. They might eventually bring about the dissolution of his marriage to Catherine, but Henry feared Wolsey would then want him to seal the Anglo-French alliance by marrying a French princess. He resolved, therefore, to take Anne's advice, and send one of his secretaries, Dr. William Knight, to ask Clement VII point blank both to allow him to marry a second time without waiting for a legal decision on the validity of his marriage to Catherine, and further, to issue a dispensation so that he could marry Anne, despite the irregular relations he had had previously with her sister, Mary. Less tender consciences might consider that if he married Anne, Henry would be committing a sin similar to the one he claimed to have committed in marrying Catherine.

But Henry's conscience, conditioned by his desire to possess Anne, perceived a significant difference. When Pope Julius II had granted the dispensation to allow him to marry Catherine, he had presumed to set aside divine law, and, by depriving Henry of a male heir, God had punished this wickedness. But now, in 1527, Henry was asking Clement VII merely to override the man-made canon law, which declared that Henry and Anne were within the prohibited limits of affinity. By similar deft reasoning and fine distinctions, Henry could unblushingly rebuke his sister, Queen Margaret, who had left her husband, the earl of Angus, for her lover, Henry Stewart. He reminded her that both the Old and the New Testament upheld the indissolubility of marriage, and condemned the mortal sin of adultery. He went on to bewail the fate of Margaret Douglas, the child of Margaret and Angus, because the dispensation by which Margaret's marriage to Angus had been declared null made her illegitimate, and he completed this apparent hypocrisy by advising Margaret to become reconciled to Angus, her 'true married husband, for during his life ye may have none other by the law of God'. To Henry this seemed sincere and sound advice. Since in the eyes of God he had never been married to Catherine, it must be patent to all that none of his own amatory adventures could be classed as adultery.

By Henry's instructions, Knight visited Wolsey at Compiègne on his way to Rome. Knight told him few of the details of his errand, but these were sufficient to send Wolsey back to England in haste and alarm. He arrived at Richmond on 30 September. Much to his embarrassment and anger, Henry refused him a private audience and required him to give his report in the presence of Anne and a group of courtiers. It was painfully clear to Wolsey that during his three months' absence in France, Anne, who disliked both him and his policies, had greatly increased her hold over the king. Visitors to court might not readily realise that Anne constituted a serious threat to the queen, for Catherine still directed the royal household, shared the royal apartments, and automatically took her rightful place on public occasions. But even the most casual visitor could see that Henry burned with desire for Anne, and that Anne presumed on it.

Despite his strained reception, Wolsey did not take long to discover the requests which Knight intended to make in Rome. He showed Henry what folly it was to ask papal permission to marry Anne before his marriage to Catherine had been declared void. Clement might very

well agree that bigamy was a lesser evil than divorce. He could ɪ
several useful precedents and numbers of theologians, including Luthe
to support Erasmus's view that he would prefer 'Jupiter' to take twċ
'Junos' rather than put one away. But Henry's subjects would detest
such action, and probably refuse to recognise the legitimacy of any
children Anne might bear him. Henry saw the sense of this, and dutifully sent his second thoughts after Knight, cancelling previous orders,
and instructing him to ask to submit the marriage problem to a legatine
court in England. In December 1527 Clement escaped from his con-
finement in St. Angelo to precarious freedom at Orvieto, some 60 miles
to the north of Rome. There he granted Knight an audience, and in the
end fobbed him off with a useless authority by which Wolsey could
try 'the king's affair' in England, and Catherine could afterwards appeal
to Rome. Wolsey, like an indulgent schoolmaster, pointed out to
Henry and Anne the defects of the documents, which their chosen
agent, with considerable self-satisfaction, had sent back from Rome.
They in turn contritely agreed that Wolsey should send off two of his
own men, Stephen Gardiner and Edward Foxe, to try again.

Gardiner and Foxe left England in mid-February 1528. Wolsey had
briefed them well, and they carried letters for the pope, in which Henry
assured Clement that 'our fidelity and reverence towards your holiness
and the Apostolic See is more firm and sure than ought to be expressed
by messengers and the testimony of letters'. He urged him to grant the
necessary dispensation because there was at stake nothing less than 'the
continuation of our succession, the quiet (as the ruin) of our kingdom,
and safety of our being'. Wolsey wrote too, and told Clement of
Henry's troubled conscience, of his continuing love for Catherine,
whom he 'minds to love and treat as his sister, with all manner of
kindness', and, for diplomacy's sake, of the outstanding virtues of Anne,
her purity, chasteness, meekness, wisdom, and her noble descent. By
3 May Foxe had hurried back to Greenwich to report success. He
delighted Henry and Anne with the news that the pope had agreed
that Wolsey and Campeggio, the two judges Henry had asked for,
should hear the king's case in London. But when Foxe delivered his
papers to Wolsey, the cardinal soon saw that Gardiner had fared little
better than Knight, in that Clement still reserved final judgment for
himself. Wolsey decided it was better to say nothing than destroy
Henry's optimistic hopes. He wrote again to Gardiner, however, asking

him to press for a decretal in which Clement would define the law so clearly that he and Campeggio would only have to judge the facts. He then composed himself to wait as patiently as possible while Campeggio, who suffered from gout, made his slow and painful way across Europe during the late-summer weeks of 1528.

Meantime, a new major worry distracted Henry's mind from his courting of Anne. Sweating sickness had returned to London, and in mid-June one of Anne's maids fell ill of it. Immediately Henry broke up court. He and Catherine rode to Waltham in Essex, and Anne, a possible contact, returned to her home at Hever. Henry was well launched on his customary convolutions to avoid the plague spots when he received word that both Anne and her father were ill. He made no attempt to visit Anne but contented himself by writing that he desired her good health as he desired his own, and that he deplored the longer absence that her illness would make necessary. Dr. Chambers, his favourite physician, was away from court, so he sent Dr. Butts to Hever to do what he could for Anne. Both Anne and her father made quick recoveries, and a few days later Butts rejoined the court, which had moved on to one of Wolsey's houses in Essex. Henry rationalised his panic by advocating a means of combating plague. In a letter to Wolsey he bade the cardinal 'keep out of all air where any of that infection is, and that if in one place anyone fall sick thereof, that Your Grace incontinently do remove to a clean place; and so, in like case, from that place to another and with a small and clean company'. Wolsey should restrict himself to small suppers, drink little wine, and take pills once a week. Should the illness strike him despite all these precautions, he should maintain a moderate sweat from the beginning 'without suffering the sweat to run in'. Henry escaped the infection, but several of his attendants caught it and had to be left behind in the continuing quest for 'a clean place'. Some recovered, but among those who died were William Carey, Anne's brother-in-law, and two of the king's close and long-standing friends, Sir Francis Poyntz and Sir William Compton.

Pestilence also struck Anglo-French hopes a cruel blow in Italy. In accordance with the treaty signed by Wolsey at Amiens, Lautrec led a large army into Italy during the early months of 1528, marched through Rome, and besieged the emperor's main forces in Naples. Clement, therefore, could hardly refuse Gardiner's request for a decretal, since he spoke on behalf of the sworn ally of Francis, Rome's deliverer. But Clement did not think that Lautrec's lightning success would end the struggle for power in Italy. He was fearful that the emperor would recover control, and accordingly instructed Campeggio to show the decretal to none but Henry and Wolsey, and in no circumstances to allow it out of his possession. His forebodings were fully justified. Before Campeggio reached England, French authority in Italy had collapsed. Lautrec and hundreds of his troops had died of plague before Naples, Charles had received unexpected help from Genoa, and the Italian states, ever-sensitive to changes in political balance, had shuffled into fresh alliances which strengthened the power of the emperor. Clement bitterly regretted having signed the decretal, and from mid-September he sent Campeggio a series of panic instructions to do nothing to anger the emperor, and to spin out proceedings as long as possible. Above all he must come to no decision about the marriage of Henry and Catherine.

Campeggio in England

Campeggio arrived in London early in October 1528. Henry, Anne and Wolsey wished to make as much haste as decency allowed, but Campeggio claiming authority to direct the legal action, exasperated them all by his slow and deliberate preliminaries. He scrupulously maintained that his first duty was to try and reconcile the two contesting parties, and in several audiences he pressed Henry to abandon the whole scheme. Henry refused, but he enjoyed having theological and legal arguments with so distinguished a canonist. He did not deny that the pope had the power of dispensation, but, he argued, Julius II had been deceived by Ferdinand of Aragon and Henry VII when he had issued the dispensation for this particular marriage. It had not been a marriage necessary for preserving peace between England and Spain as had been alleged, and certainly he, only 12 years of age at that time, had never asked for it. On the contrary, two years later he had publicly objected to it. Since then God had given signal proof that He too disapproved. Campeggio's answers and suggestions all fell on closed ears: not even an angel from heaven, he declared, could turn Henry from his own interpretation of the facts. He was equally unsuccessful when he tried to persuade Catherine to follow the example of Jeanne, the first wife of Louis XII, who had gone into a nunnery so that her husband could make a politically important marriage with Anne of Brittany. Henry grasped eagerly at the suggestion of Catherine entering a nunnery, but she stubbornly stuck to her first simple statement that she and Arthur had never consummated their marriage. On this point her conscience, pricked by fears of what might befall Mary, proved as tender as Henry's. Campeggio thankfully accepted Catherine's statement as good reason for further delay. If she were right—and who but Henry could say that she was not?—Campeggio maintained that the investigation was closed. But Wolsey's agile mind produced a complicated argument to show that Henry still had a genuine case to put before the legatine court.

Meantime, Henry awoke to a belated realisation that the Londoners disliked this investigation. Eight months before, he had intervened to prevent 'Wolsey's war' jeopardising trade between England and the Netherlands, and in June, to the Londoners' relief, he had signed a formal truce with Charles. London had acquired the habit of blaming Wolsey for all its misfortunes, and now in the autumn of 1528 its citizens greeted him and the French ambassador with catcalls, and Catherine with cheers and expressions of sympathy. As Hall expressed it, 'in especial, women and other that favored the quene talked largely'. Consequently Henry decided it would be prudent to look to his public relations. On 8 November he spoke to a crowded audience of nobles, judges, aldermen, and others in the palace of Bridewell, and after reminding them of the blessings of peace and prosperity they had enjoyed during the last twenty years, he declared that all would be endangered if he left no heir to succeed him. 'And although it hath pleased almighty God to send us a fayre doughter of a noble woman and me begotten to our great comfort and joy, yet it hath been told us by diverse great clerkes, that neither she is our lawful doughter nor her mother our lawful wyfe.' For this reason it had been necessary to seek the advice of the greatest clerks in Christendom. Should they decide that Catherine was still his wife 'there was never thinge more pleasaunt nor more acceptable to me in my lyfe', for '(as you wel know) she is a woman of moste gentlenes, of most humilitie and buxumnes, yea and of al good qualities apperteignynge to nobilitie, she is wythoute comparyson, as I this xx yeres almoste have had the true experiment, so that yf I were to mary agayne if the mariage myght be good I would surely chose her above al other women'. But if the judgment was that

Catherine was not his wife, then he would lament to have lived so long in adultery. 'These bee the sores that vexe my minde.' Henry ended by bidding the members of his audience make widely known the true reasons for the presence of the legates in London. It is unlikely, however, that this specious vindication, some of it humbug to mollify the friends of Catherine, changed the inmost thoughts of many people. Even the loyal Hall commented that 'some syghed and sayd nothynge' and that 'every man spake as his hert served him'. Most Londoners probably considered that Henry's troubled conscience, genuine though it might be, was all part of the foxy Wolsey's plans to strengthen the hated French alliance.

When he spoke at Bridewell Henry had good hopes that Campeggio and Wolsey would begin formally to hear evidence before Christmas 1528. But everything was thrown into fresh confusion by the discovery of a brief which Pope Julius had issued along with the original dispensation, and which friends of Catherine had recently found among the private papers of de Puebla the Spanish ambassador who had negotiated her marriage. The careful phrasing of this new document answered all objections which Henry's legal representatives had made against the dispensation. It had quite as much legal authority as the dispensation, and Charles V had no intention of letting so valuable a document out of his custody. He allowed two English ambassadors to examine it, and sent an attested copy to Mendoza, his own ambassador in England. But he would go no further. Henry impetuously proclaimed the brief a forgery, and sent envoys to Rome demanding that the pope should denounce it. With evident reason Clement replied simply by asking how he could declare a document a forgery without having first seen it. All this arguing, coming, and going wasted precious weeks. Each day convinced Clement the more that he dared not offend Charles, and increasingly tempted him to recall Campeggio and try the case in Rome. Gardiner warned Henry that this danger was imminent, and he and Wolsey decided to ignore the brief and compel Campeggio to open the London hearing.

The court met at Blackfriars. On 18 June Catherine questioned its competency to judge the case, and three days later she and Henry went to Blackfriars to hear the court's judgment on this point. It was an odd, Gilbertian spectacle. Drs. Sampson and Bell represented Henry on the floor of the court, but the defendant himself was enthroned above the judges on the right on 'a chayer and cushyons of ryche Tyssue'. On the other side of the court and also raised above the judges sat Queen Catherine on another 'ryche chayer'. Her counsel included Warham himself, and the bishops of London, Bath and Wells, Rochester, and St. Asaph. Yet out of this imposing array only Fisher of Rochester 'stode stiffe in her cause'. The remainder bent before Henry's wishes, for, as the old archbishop once mumbled in Catherine's ear, to provoke the wrath of a king meant death. Henry answered his formal calling with a resounding 'Here I am', but when the court usher called Catherine she walked across the court, knelt before Henry and made a last moving appeal that he would put an end to it all. In everyone's hearing she confessed her love and loyalty to him, and claimed that he knew as well as she did that she had come to him 'a true maid, without touch of man'. The embarrassed Henry tried to assure her that he would be most happy if the court pronounced their marriage valid, but that the case must go on, and certainly could not be transferred to Rome. These words in no way deterred Catherine. Without a sign that she recognised the presence of the legates, she quietly walked out of the hall. The court had no option but to proceed without her.

While Campeggio and Wolsey listened day after day at Blackfriars to evidence which was plentiful but mostly irrelevant, and Fisher did what he could on Catherine's behalf, Anglo-French prestige in Italy deteriorated into ruin. Henry failed to persuade his ally, Venice, to surrender two papal towns which she had seized, and on 21 June French arms suffered a major defeat at Landriano in northern Italy. A week later Clement thankfully made his peace with Charles V by signing the treaty of Barcelona, one clause of which stipulated that the legatine court in London should be dissolved. Secretly warned of what was about to happen, Wolsey determined to bring the hearing of evidence to an end and have judgment given. But Campeggio outwitted him. He too may have been warned, or he may have sensed from Wolsey's new impatience what was happening in Rome. On 23 July Henry and his courtiers assembled to hear the verdict, but their mouths opened with astonishment when Campeggio calmly announced that since his court was part of the court of Rome, he was obliged to observe Roman rules and tradition. Consequently he was standing the court adjourned until the new term, which would open on 1 October. The shock and disappointment common to all found voice in Charles Brandon, who blurted out, 'It was never merry in England whilst we had cardinals among us'. A few days later Henry received official confirmation that Clement had called the case to Rome, and learned that at Cambrai Francis had made his peace with Charles V, and so abandoned any further plans to break or reduce Imperial authority in Italy.

These accumulating disappointments made Henry very angry. But worse still they left him baffled and bewildered, because he had no clear idea what to do next. Normally he would have expected Wolsey to argue out with him a reasoned statement of the new situation, but Wolsey had been the sole architect of this double disaster. It was he who had convinced him that he had tied England and France 'in suche a perfite knot that it shall never fayle': yet, as soon as it suited French interests to do so, Francis had deserted him. It was he who had insisted that a legatine court was the surest way of putting Catherine aside: yet, although he enjoyed considerable ecclesiastical authority, he had failed to persuade his fellow legate to pronounce the obvious verdict. Indeed, so far had Wolsey failed his king, that Campeggio might even be returning to Rome unconvinced of the legal strength of Henry's case. During long years of close association Henry had known Wolsey make several mistakes of judgment, but never so disastrously as this. It might well be that Anne, Norfolk, and Suffolk were right, when they suggested that what Wolsey lacked in handling the marriage problem was not skill but will.

From the beginning Anne had mistrusted Wolsey. She was convinced that he despised her and was resolved to bar her way to the throne. But so long as he had power and Henry had faith in the efficiency of the legatine court, she was prepared to flatter him and outwardly respect his position. She wrote to him submissively and without any trace of hostility, wishing him on one occasion 'much increase of honour with long life', and on another 'good health and prosperity as the writer would'. Campeggio's arrival in England increased Anne's forebodings of failure, but she took comfort from the fine style in which Henry lodged her at court during Christmas 1528, and from the open way he paraded his intention to make her his queen. She made no difficulties about staying away from court while the tribunal was sitting, but once Campeggio announced the adjournment she vented her long-suppressed anger on Wolsey. Henry mollified her a little by taking her with him first to Greenwich and then on his usual summer hunting tour. He pleased her further by declining to grant Wolsey an audience, and possibly increased her confidence when he issued writs for parliament to meet in the autumn. During Wolsey's period of power, parliament had ceased to be a regular feature of English government. Henry turned to it now primarily in expectation of receiving money, and secondly because there was always a possibility that it might produce fruitful ideas. But many of his subjects must have taken the election writs as a declaration that the age of Wolsey was over. Certainly Henry had no real faith in Wolsey any longer, but he did not share the view of Anne and her friends that he could immediately discard him. They advocated ignoring Rome, but Henry could see no satisfactory way to his new marriage except by papal authority. He could not believe that Clement opposed his reasonable request on principle. He would grant the dispensation once Henry could reduce or outbid Imperial influence in Rome, but it would not bring that day nearer if Henry and his ministers insulted Clement's representatives. Therefore, in mid-September, after many long enjoyable days of hunting in Oxfordshire, Northamptonshire, and Essex had dissipated his immediate anger and hostility, Henry agreed to receive the two cardinals at Grafton before Campeggio left for Rome. To the surprise of his courtiers and the anger of Anne and her friends, he showed particular friendship towards Wolsey. He had a few words in private with him both before and after dinner, but next morning he rode off early with Anne for a day's sport, and Wolsey accompanied Campeggio back to London. On 8 October Campeggio arrived at Dover. The customs officers ransacked his luggage, but York herald, Campeggio's escort from London to Dover, returned with the sad news that the officers had found nothing but old clothes and soiled linen. Campeggio carried neither the treasure, which rumour reported Wolsey had given him to put in safe keeping on the Continent, nor the decretal, by which, Henry had persuaded himself, Wolsey could still 'legally' annul the marriage. Depressed by this new disappointment, Henry no longer troubled to hold back Wolsey's enemies.

Changes in Council

On 9 October the attorney-general prepared a bill of indictment against Wolsey, and two days later the dukes of Norfolk and Suffolk jointly required him to surrender to them the great seal. Wolsey proudly refused until they could bring him an authority signed by the king, but the sight of Henry's signature on the writ reduced him to tears. He, like many others, automatically assumed he was a con-demned man. Abjectly he acknowledged that holding a papal court in England broke the statute of praemunire, and he tried to placate and distract his accusers by giving pensions to several friends of Anne, and by surrendering to Henry considerable treasure in money and goods including York House, later to be known as Whitehall. When, much to his surprise, the humbled, stricken cardinal found himself still at liberty, he rode to Esher, and during the next few weeks endured a spartan existence in the ill-furnished house, which he controlled in his capacity as bishop of Winchester.

Meantime, Henry had started another hare. Early in August, Gardiner and Foxe had retailed to him the opinion recently advanced by Thomas Cranmer, a Cambridge acquaintance of theirs, that he should ask the universities of Europe for their opinion on the legality of his marriage. Henry jumped at the idea—'That man hath the right sow by the ear'. It would take considerable time to gather together the judgments of the different universities, but a favourable verdict from a majority of the learned men of Christendom would be almost papal in authority, and give him either a powerful weapon with which to belabour the pope, or a remarkable justification if in the end circumstances drove him to go his own way. At the very least it meant action, and both he and Anne felt better when they knew that someone was doing something, however unhopeful, to bring about their legal union. From Cambridge and Oxford royal agents obtained guarded statements that the marriage between Henry and Catherine had been illegal, and throughout 1530 other academic ambassadors were busy in the Continental universities. With the blessing and help of Francis I they achieved surprising success, and would have done better still if the emperor's agents had not countered their work. Several French and Italian universities, including Paris, Bourges, Bologna and Padua, were induced to declare for Henry. His chief opponents were the Spanish universities, which dared not declare against a princess of Aragon, and those German universities in which Lutheranism was strong. Henry sought Luther's own opinion through a self-exiled disciple, Robert Barnes, formerly prior of the Augustinian house at Cambridge. Luther took the trouble to set out his judgment in a long, detailed treatise, in which he argued that the injunction in *Deuteronomy* applied to Henry because the ban in *Leviticus* only concerned cases in which the bridegroom's brother was living at the time of the second marriage. Herod had sinfully taken Herodias because his brother, Philip, still lived, but Henry had obeyed, and not broken, the law when he had married Catherine.⌉

In the new executive which Henry had to create after Wolsey had been dismissed, Norfolk, Anne's uncle, became president of the council, and Suffolk, Henry's brother-in-law, vice-president. Their friend, Sir William Fitzwilliam, combined the treasurership of the household with the chancellorship of the duchy of Lancaster. A few months later, Tunstal, a mild supporter of Catherine but an able royal diplomat, went north to the rich see of Durham, and left the bishopric of London to John Stokesley, an advocate of Anne, and the privy seal to Anne's father, lately raised further to the dignity of earl of Wiltshire and Ormond. In harness with these incompatible colleagues, Henry insisted that Thomas More should serve him as chancellor. More would have declined the honour and responsibility could he have done so, for, since he had always quietly but consistently taken Catherine's part, he knew that his tenure of office could easily end as disastrously as Wolsey's. But the king refused to have another cleric and instinctively shied at a noble chancellor, who almost certainly would misuse his office to advance his family's fortunes and endanger the independence and exaltation of the crown which he and his father had achieved. His chancellor must be a man of ideas capable of suggesting policies that after examination Henry could either accept or reject. He must be trustworthy, able to transact routine business and make executive decisions, for Henry had still no intention of wasting hunting and pleasure-seeking days on tedious paper or judicial work. He considered that More would give him as faithful service and as wise advice as Wolsey had ever done, and that unlike Wolsey he would not be distracted from a single-minded devotion to the crown by loyalty to other vows. He would speak his mind on matters of policy, and by argument would enable his king to make good decisions. Henry knew that More did not yet approve of his desire to have his marriage declared null. On that matter he agreed that his new chancellor 'should first look unto God, and after God unto him'. But he had little doubt that before long More was bound to recognise the reasonableness of his king's arguments.

On 3 November 1529, less than a week after he had received the great seal, More stood by Henry's side in the hall at Blackfriars, and in the king's name welcomed the lords and commons to the new parliament. He spoke of Henry as the good, ever vigilant shepherd, who, for the well-being of his flock, had recently thrust out 'the great wether', which had presumed that the shepherd 'had no wit to perceive his craftie doyng'. Wolsey had made a pitiable mistake, 'for his grace's sight was so quicke and penetrable, that he saw him, yea and saw through him, both within and without, so that all thing to him was open, and accordyng to his desert he hath had a gentle correction, which smal ponishment the kynge will not to be an example to other offendoures'. Henry declared somewhat vaguely that his purpose in calling parliament was to reform 'divers new enormities' which had appeared among the people and for which the law had no remedy, and he soon made it clear that he required money and would like to be released from repaying the £150,000 which Wolsey had borrowed for him from many of his subjects. On their side most members of the commons had strong views, not all of which suited Henry's purpose. Like their predecessors they showed no eagerness to authorise taxation. They were still nervous about the future of trade with the Netherlands, and therefore preferred Henry to lean towards the emperor rather than towards Francis. They had a chivalrous respect for Queen Catherine, and chiefly for this reason liked the Boleyn faction little better than they had liked Wolsey. They nursed chronic grudges and grievances against the exactions and privileges of the clergy, and they bridled to think that two legates had dared to sit in judgment on their king, and that the pope had had the temerity to recall Henry's case to Rome. In Henry's eyes these deep, widespread feelings among the representatives of his subjects seemed muddle-headed and contradictory, but with sympathetic handling, clever advice, and some clumsy bungling in Rome, he used these very sentiments and prejudices during the next three years to achieve his immediate objectives and incidentally revolutionise England's position in Christendom.

In the first session the commons introduced bills to limit clerical fees for probate and mortuaries, to reduce absenteeism and pluralities in the church, and to prevent clergy from trading. When the lords discussed these bills the bishops demanded that they should be thrown out, and Fisher blamed the anti-clericalism of 'the Common house' on 'lack of faith'. The commons resented this, and the speaker, Thomas Audeley, protested so strongly that Fisher withdrew his remark. Henry wanted the bills to become law, so he suggested that a small committee of both houses should decide the issue between the lords and commons. As he anticipated, the lay lords sided with the commoners to outvote the bishops, and the bills were presented for his signature. This first skirmish had worsted the church, but Henry had not got all his own way. The commons had relieved him of his debts but had neither voted the taxation he would have liked, nor considered his bill of wills and uses, by which he had hoped to strengthen the feudal rights of the crown.

A week before he prorogued parliament on 16 December 1529, Henry gave a banquet to celebrate Anne's new dignity as Lady Anne Rochford. Catherine was still at court. She steadfastly refused either to join her daughter or to retire to some quiet refuge, and Henry still could not bring himself to insist. Consequently he spent many uncomfortable hours, for Catherine, who still did such wifely duties as supervising the making and laundering of his linen, and whom he still sometimes saw privately, scorned his conscientious scruples, and Anne constantly complained that he was wasting her youth and that he took no steps to marry her. Even absolute monarchy gives a man no immunity against such female pressures. Henry tried to please both his ladies in turn. Catherine did not attend the December banquet, and, to her own satisfaction but to the disgust of the duchesses of Norfolk and Suffolk, Anne was given pride of place. But at the Christmas festivities Catherine took her usual seat and Anne did not appear. Throughout 1530 Henry vacillated between ignoring Catherine for weeks at a time as he did early in the year, and keeping her at his side as he did during one of his summer progresses. The Boleyns were not popular at court. Their display of pride in their success made them many enemies, and it was with relief that Norfolk and Suffolk saw Anne's father set out on a forlorn mission to Italy on 21 January 1530. Henry still thirsted for action, but however desperate he was to feel that he was doing something to bring about his marriage to Anne, he could scarcely have soberly expected Wiltshire to bring back success. At Bologna the pope was due to crown Charles V emperor, and the jaunty, inexperienced Wiltshire was required to seize this unpromising opportunity to persuade Charles to withdraw his objections and allow Clement to issue the much disputed dispensation. Charles laughed at him. Papal officers increased his discomfiture by serving on him the writ summoni Henry to appear before the Rota, the supreme court at Rome, and Wiltshire only saved face by returning to England through Paris, and bringing with him the favourable reports from the French and northern-Italian universities.

Close on his heels came Jean du Bellay, a French bishop and special envoy from Francis. He boldly proposed that Henry should take the law into his own hands and marry Anne, for he was confident that once Anne was queen, the combined pressure of Francis and Henry at Rome would compel Clement to ratify the marriage. But only Norfolk, Fitzwilliam, and Wiltshire advised Henry to do this. The remainder of Henry's councillors either had no wish to see Anne queen, or rightly suspected that du Bellay's chief concern was to make permanent Henry's dependence on France and the division between Henry and Charles. Moreover, so unorthodox a proposal made no appeal to Henry. His great reverence for legal forms could not easily stomach retrospective approval. One of the grounds for du Bellay's argument was that in March 1530 Gabriel de Grammont, bishop of Tarbes, had declared to Francis that 'more than three times in secret' Clement had told him he would be happy if Henry would marry Anne either on the authority of Wolsey's legatine powers or any other authority that would not involve Rome directly. In September 1530, Gregory Casale, one of Henry's permanent representatives at Rome, partially confirmed this report when he wrote that Clement had secretly suggested to him that Henry should take two wives by marrying Anne before any decision had been reached about his marriage to Catherine. But in his formal announcements Clement spoke with a very different voice. In a series of bulls dating from March 1530 to the following January he threatened excommunication if Henry dared marry Anne without legal sanction. He forbade him to live with any other woman but Catherine, and warned all women against going through a marriage ceremony with him. For good measure, he later prohibited anyone from speaking or writing against the validity of Catherine's marriage, or any court or other body from attempting to pass judgment on it. Clement's purpose in issuing these unnecessary strictures was probably to please his ally and political master the emperor, but in doing so he increased anti-papal feeling in England, and stung Henry into outraged defence of his own prerogative. Once again he reached for the statute of praemunire, the all-purpose weapon which Chapuys, the new Imperial ambassador in London, slyly declared he limited or amplified according to his will and applied to anyone he pleased. In September 1530 he proclaimed to his subjects and privately informed the papal nuncio that English law determined that those who brought into England papal bulls touching 'our Lord the King, against him, his crown, and his royalty, or his realm', or those who made 'thereof notification' should be 'put out of the king's protection, and their lands, tenements, goods, and chattels forefeited to our Lord the King, and that they be attached by their bodies . . . and brought before the King and his Council'.

This statute, passed so long ago as 1393, pleased the increasing number of Englishmen who were saying a little wildly that England should go her own way heedless of praise or blame from across the Channel, and unfettered by the moral and economic chains by which Rome profitably kept western Christendom together. The same law had been the technical reason for Wolsey's downfall, for it was no defence to plead that Wolsey had been exercising papal jurisdiction in England with Henry's consent and in order to fulfil Henry's declared policy. Wolsey's many enemies only wished that the king would bring him to trial and exact the full legal penalty. Instead, Henry, temporarily relieved of his most pressing debts by the treasure Wolsey had surrendered to him, pardoned the cardinal and seemed to be content to allow him to ingratiate himself with the people of the province of York. It was quite possible that Henry might recall Wolsey to the council, for the king had met little success and had followed no enterprising or promising policy since Wolsey had ceased to be chief minister. This threatened danger brought the squabbling ministers together, and by the end of October 1530 they managed to put before Henry evidence which suggested that Wolsey had been attempting to intrigue with the French and Italian ambassadors against the king's ministers, and had been encouraging Clement to denounce Henry's proposed marriage with Anne. On 4 November the earl of Northumberland, Anne's one-time admirer, arrested Wolsey in the king's name, but three weeks later, when the prisoner and his escort had travelled no further than Leicester, Wolsey died. By odd coincidence the body of this proud, ambitious, capable man was interred in Leicester Abbey, not far from Greyfriars Church in which Richard III lies buried. Both cardinal and king possessed unusual talents, and both in their time had shown unshakeable loyalty to their sovereign lords, Henry VIII and Edward IV. Yet neither had sufficiently regarded the reaction of lesser men to their aggressive, self-justified policies. They had made numerous lively and strong enemies, many of whom had ample justification for their hatred, even if at the end of their lives both Wolsey and Richard could with some reason echo Job's lament, 'Behold, I cry out of wrong but I am not heard: I cry for help but there is no judgment'. Sixteenth-century England condemned both men as tyrants.

Henry did not mourn for Wolsey—he was too self-absorbed for that—but often in 1529 and 1530 he must have looked back with affection on the days when life had been simpler, and with confidence and ease of mind he had left to Wolsey the routine problems of government. His new ministers were neither so inventive nor so hard-working as Wolsey. On the marriage problem they did not seem to have a new, acceptable idea between them. Thomas More was an efficient enough chancellor, but on this key issue refused to give advice. Gardiner, the capable, astute secretary, seemed content to wait indefinitely for Rome to give its verdict. Norfolk and Suffolk showed no interest in Henry's predicament, and Anne and her friends advocated wild, impossible solutions such as committing bigamy or following Luther's example and severing England's connection with Rome. Henry himself could see no way ahead. If he sent Anne from court and returned to the calm routine of life with Catherine, he still had no prospect of a son to succeed him. If he married Anne, he would almost certainly make Charles V an enemy for life, inevitably encounter strong opposition in England, and, most unwelcome thought, hurt Catherine beyond reconciliation. Unsatisfied desire for Anne led him to prefer the second alternative, but he could see no way round Clement's consistent refusal to grant the dispensation which alone could make his second marriage legal. And Henry insisted upon legality, however specious or contrived. Instinctively he recoiled from all illegal actions, and in addition he realised that unless his second marriage satisfied the letter of the law, the son whom Anne would bear him would be barred from the throne.

In this bewilderment Henry first heard the persuasive, confident voice of Thomas Cromwell. 'The autumn of 1530' is the most exact date it is possible to give for the beginning of their close association. A prospect of finding more money for the treasury brought them together. As a zealous servant for Wolsey, Cromwell had helped Dr. John Allen to suppress a score of 'exile and small monasteries' in order that their revenues could finance the building of Cardinal's College at Oxford, and after Wolsey's fall he had used such money and assets as the cardinal retained avowedly to hold back his master's most revengeful enemies, but primarily to buy his way into the new circle of power. In the first session of the Reformation Parliament he had persuaded the commons to reject the lord's bill of attainder against Wolsey, and in February 1530 had gained his master a formal pardon under the great seal. Nevertheless, he looked steadily to his own future, and therefore helped Henry to take over the revenues of the forfeited sees of St. Albans and Winchester, and plunder the income of Wolsey's colleges at Oxford and Ipswich. By the time Wolsey died, Henry already realised Cromwell's value. He did not give him a seat in the council immediately, but increasing new thrust and purpose in Henry's policy usually betrays Cromwell's presence near the throne.

Henry's signature

4 SEPARATION FROM ROME

By the mass, Master More, it is perilous striving with princes. And therefore, I would wish you somewhat to incline to the King's pleasure, for by God's body, Master More, Indignatio principis mors est.

DUKE OF NORFOLK as reported by WILLIAM ROPER

PARLIAMENT met again in January 1531. Plague and indecision had caused Henry to postpone arranged meetings two or three times in 1530, but in unsuitable January weather lords and commons eventually gathered at Westminster Palace. About the same time the convocation of Canterbury met in considerable dread at the Abbey. During previous weeks a number of church leaders had been accused of breaking the statute of praemunire by having recognised Wolsey's authority as legate, and in December the attorney-general had extended these individual charges into a general indictment of all clergy. Convocation, like Wolsey, realised it was impossible to fight against the statute, and considered it would be simpler and cheaper to yield to the blackmail and buy itself a pardon. Henry always needed more money, and would hardly refuse a substantial sum. It offered £40,000, but Henry required at least £100,000. Convocation reluctantly agreed, only to find itself faced with the further demand that it should formally acknowledge its grievous offence and recognise the king as 'sole protector and Supreme Head of the Church and clergy of England'. To many clerics and not a few laymen this was a more serious matter than the fine. Some could not find among the many interpretations of this new title any acceptable one which did not diminish papal supremacy. Nevertheless, all clergy were grimly aware of the dark shadow of the statute which still hung over them, and after considerable discussion and further consultation with Henry, Warham gladly took silence for consent when he proposed the modified title of 'singular protector, only and supreme lord, and, as far as the law of Christ allows, even

Supreme Head'. York convocation faced the same demands as Canterbury, except that the poorer province had to pay considerably less—£19,000. In the absence of an archbishop, Tunstal of Durham presided, and resisted until May 1531 before consenting to the required title. He proposed 'Only and Supreme Lord after Christ in Temporal Matters', but Henry rejected this in a long letter which obviously he enjoyed writing. Theological argument always attracted him, and here he worked out his case clause by clause and came near to a precise interpretation of the title. He assured Tunstal that he sought power not over spiritual things but over spiritual persons, and that his new title would hardly extend his existing powers over church property, church courts, or the appointment of clergy. Convocation of York submitted, but Tunstal insisted that the clerk officially recorded his personal protest.

Henry embodied his victory over the clergy in an act of parliament in which phrases flattering to the kindness and magnanimity of the crown, almost, but not quite, smothered such business-like sentences as 'subsidy of one hundred thousand pounds of lawful money current in this realm, to be levied and collected by the said clergy at their proper costs and charges'. An act which required other people to pay money to the crown and at the same time pandered to the anti-clerical sentiments of many members could not fail to gratify the commons. Yet before they would vote for it, Henry 'moved with most tender pity, love, and compassion', had to promise to grant to 'his temporal and lay subjects . . . his most gracious, general, and free pardon'. For 'divers froward' members readily understood that the very arguments which the bill used against the clergy could be aimed with equally devastating effects at all laymen who had co-operated actively or passively with Wolsey. Henry granted the pardon willingly enough. Clerical power was his quarry, and the pardon was a small price to pay if it brought parliament enthusiastically into the hunt.

Nine months of frustration followed immediately upon this burst of activity and show of regal power. At the end of March Henry sent Sir Brian Tuke, his treasurer of the household, to the lords to read a long statement upon 'the king's great matter'. He repeated the old arguments and reminded their lordships of the favourable opinions given by a dozen universities. Longland and Stokesley, bishops of Lincoln and London, made supporting speeches, but no sooner had they finished than the bishops of Bath and St. Asaph led a devastating counter-attack. Tuke withdrew in some discomfiture. In the commons he fared no better. Members heard him in silence and offered no comment at all. Henry accepted the rebuff and prorogued parliament.

Fortunately for Henry the remaining months of 1531 failed to advance Catherine's cause any more than his own. The queen could draw comfort from her popularity among the Londoners, from parliament's apparent indifference to the pricks of Henry's conscience, and particularly from the opinion lately expressed by archbishop Warham, not notable for his courage, that the papal interdict effectively prevented his court at Canterbury from hearing the king's plea against the validity of his marriage. Yet though she suffered no defeat, she gained no victory. She, who knew Henry as well as anyone, had long advocated that the pope should resolutely declare her marriage valid and forbid Henry under pain of excommunication to commit bigamy. This boldness would provoke Henry to violent outbursts of anger and defiant speeches, but, she believed, it was the only way of waking Henry from his dream of begetting heirs by Anne, and the quickest way of bringing the whole deplorable affair to a satisfactory solution. Henry would not risk excommunication. Yet, instead of attacking, Clement was stalling. He had called the case to Rome in the summer of 1529, but two wasted years later the court had not even met. In Catherine's view this was most dangerous, for, as she rightly surmised, time favoured Anne and not herself. Papal indecision and vacillation only strengthened Henry in his belief that his conscience spoke the truth, and exasperated him into wild thoughts of acting on his own. Moreover, the apparent lofty indifference of Rome to Henry's wishes provided useful propaganda for those in England who detested Rome's power and influence. 'If the Pope grants further delay, as the King of France is said to have requested', wrote Catherine to Charles in April 1531, 'you can expect that before long these people will achieve all they are aiming at.' But Clement did not enjoy the advantage of Catherine's single-mindedness. Luther's success in Germany, the possibility of being faced by a general council of the church, Henry's veiled threats to defy him, and the uncertainty about French policy, all frightened him into excessive caution. However, in the spring of 1531 he ventured a step forward. He wrote to Henry that he could not delay the Rome hearing much longer, and that he required Henry to appear either in person or by proxy. Henry considered this summons in council, but all that council could advise was that a deputation should once again try to persuade Catherine to withdraw her suit from Rome. It was labour in vain. The queen told Norfolk, who led the large, imposing delegation, that though she expected no favours from Clement and though she had no wish to embarrass Henry, she believed that no one could give her justice except the vicar of Christ, 'the mirror image of eternal Truth'. With a dig at Henry's well-publicised conscience, Suffolk chipped into Norfolk's report with the remark that the queen would obey the king in all things except those which offended God and her conscience. Nothing seemed capable of shaking Catherine's calm courage, which her disappointed, balked husband considered to be callous indifference to his happiness and peace of mind.

In the middle of June 1531, a fortnight after Catherine's interview with Norfolk's delegation, the court moved from Greenwich to Windsor, and on 11 July, without warning or a simple farewell to the queen, Henry and Anne rode off to live elsewhere. A month or so later, Henry sent Catherine formal instructions to move from Windsor to the More, Wolsey's old house between Beaconsfield and Watford. There she had to settle down with her small household. To the outside world she showed a calm and dignified face, but her letters and the comments of Chapuys, her chief adviser, betray how keenly she felt this latest triumph of Lady Anne, who not only kept her from court but also spitefully insisted that Henry forbade Princess Mary to visit her. She put all the blame for her tribulations on Anne's determination to push Henry headlong into heresy and disobedience of Rome. For Henry she felt sorrow rather than anger. Henry himself was not without misgivings. The hints Chapuys let fall about the emperor's preparations for war and for restricting England's trade with the Netherlands disturbed him, and he rarely met anyone except Anne and her immediate family who showed enthusiasm for the dissolution of his marriage to Catherine. He failed to see that Anne's rudeness and pride made new enemies every day, and was incensed when clerics like Gardiner and Lee and courtiers like Nicholas Carew and Thomas Elyot, all loyal servants of the crown, either counselled caution or definitely opposed all action against the queen. In October 1531, hoping against hope, he sent another deputation to see Catherine, but as he must have expected, separation had not weakened her resistance against threats or cajolery. By the end of the year Henry had convinced himself that restrained and reasonable use of his royal authority had achieved nothing, and that he must brace himself to accept Cromwell's guidance and 'make or mar' his future. Significantly, Cromwell moved from the shadows of secret meetings and a back seat in the council to the full light of a place among the most trusted of the royal ministers.

Henry and Anne spent the Christmas of 1531 at Greenwich. They took pains to impress with lavish entertainment Giles de la Pommeraye, the new ambassador whom Francis had sent over to negotiate a treaty, but, Hall, despite his loyalty and admiration for Henry, reported that 'all men sayde that there was no myrthe in that Christemas because the Queene and the Ladies were absent'. At the More, Catherine made as happy a Christmas as she could for her ladies-in-waiting, but in the privacy of her room she wept that she and Henry were parted.

Anne's Triumph

Parliament reassembled on 15 January 1532. Henry found docility neither in lords nor commons. Most of the bishops, including Warham, opposed a proposition that an English ecclesiastical court should hear the evidence against the marriage, and when, through Norfolk, Henry tested the reaction of the upper house with a suggestion that matrimonial causes should go before temporal courts, Lord Darcy, no particular friend of the church, spoke strongly against it. The commons refused to grant anything like the amount of money Henry asked for, still rejected his bill of wills and uses, and accorded a hum of approval to one member who had the temerity to say that the king would have no worry about the cost of national defence if he returned to live with Queen Catherine. Into such an independent body of men, Cromwell introduced a petition complaining of a dozen clerical abuses commonly found in diocese and parish. This was many members' pet subject, and in March, after debating the topic at some length, the commons placed before Henry its 'Supplication against the Ordinaries'. Its most serious complaint was that convocation made laws without royal or parliamentary consent, and it asked that this wrong should be put right by Henry, 'in whom and by whom the only and sole redress, reformation, and remedy herein absolutely rests and remains'.

Henry was overjoyed that once again he had gained the alliance of the commons against the bishops, but pretending his 'indifference' he passed the complaints to convocation for its comments. By the end of April he was able to hand Mr. Speaker convocation's long and detailed reply with the words, 'We think their answer will smally please you, for it seemeth to us very slender'. The commons took the hint, and refused to be satisfied. By 10 May charge and counter-charge had reached a crisis. Henry demanded that convocation should accept three articles, which would destroy the independence of the church by requiring the crown to license all canons passed by convocation, and by empowering the crown to review all existing canons. On the next day Henry explained to the speaker and a delegation from the commons what he had done, and with naïve astonishment revealed to them what he and they had known all their lives, that 'all the prelates at their consecration make an oath to the pope clean contrary to the oath they make to us, so that they seem his subjects not ours'. Dutifully, members of the commons expressed surprise and horror when the two oaths taken by the bishops were read to them, and in this strong anti-clerical atmosphere convocation surrendered more abjectly than it had done the previous year. It trusted, so it said, in Henry's 'most excellent wisdom, princely goodness, and fervent zeal for the promotions of God, honour and Christian religion, and also in his learning far exceeding in our judgment the learning of all other kings and princes we have read of'. At least one man immediately realised the full import of this surrender. Sir Thomas More resigned the great seal on 16 May, the day after convocation had made its submission.

At the same time that Henry was abetting this duel between commons and convocation, he was encouraging the lords to legislate against the payment of annates, those 'great and inestimable sums of money', as the preamble to the act exaggerated, which were 'daily conveyed out of this realm to the impoverishment of the same'. These fees which bishops paid to Rome at their consecration had long been unpopular, but Henry had to put on every pressure, including being present when the commons divided on the issue, before the bill passed both houses. The final draft was cunningly but cautiously constructed. It suspended the operation of the act until confirmed by letters patent from the king, so that in Rome, Henry could pretend he was risking unpopularity by defending the papacy against parliament. 'Whenever the statute is mentioned', he instructed his men in Rome, 'you shall instil into their ears how incessant have been our efforts to resist the importunity of our

16   SIR THOMAS MORE
*Detail of the drawing by
Hans Holbein; reproduced
by gracious permission of
H.M. The Queen*

17   JOHN FISHER
*From a contemporary copy
of a portrait by Hans
Holbein*

18   HENRY VIII
From the portrait by Hans Holbein, 1542

people from passing the statute.' The act anticipated any retaliation
from Rome by setting up legal machinery for the consecration of
bishops and archbishops without the need of papal bulls, and by
denying the efficacy of excommunication and interdict 'albeit that our
said Sovereign Lord the King and all his natural subjects as well spiritual
as temporal be as obedient, devout, Catholic and humble children of
God and Holy Church as any people be within any realm christened'.
The economic pressure which the act made it possible for Henry to
threaten to use had little apparent effect in Rome, but the changes which
the act made in English law opened the way for Cromwell to plan his
final legal campaign.

All this parliamentary activity was smilingly applauded by Francis I.
During these critical months, Henry diplomatically paid the Imperial
ambassador marked courtesy, but with the French ambassador his
ministers negotiated seriously. In April 1532 at Greenwich Lord
Wiltshire and Edward Foxe formally signed with de la Pommeraye a
treaty by which, in the event of the emperor making war, Henry and
Francis promised to aid each other on land and sea. Neither king could
afford to be indifferent. If his dispute with Rome led to war with Charles,
Henry would need as strong a Continental ally as he could get: Francis,
convinced that war was inevitable between himself and Charles, considered this treaty a surer and cheaper way of holding England than
the traditional policy of paying pensions to uncertain friends at court.
Chiefly to please Henry, both Francis and Cardinal Grammont wrote
to the pope urging him to grant the dispensation. At the same time Dr.
Ortiz, the emperor's representative in Rome, pressed Clement to ex-
communicate Henry unless he cast off his 'concubine'. As before the
pope did nothing decisive. Through his nuncio in London, he merely
requested Henry to take Catherine back into his household, a request
which Henry brushed aside without much thought. It was a minor
irritation among many. Almost daily he received reports of some
impetuous, troubled soul speaking out in favour of Catherine or
demonstrating against Anne. At Greenwich he and his courtiers listened
to William Peto, the provincial of his favourite order of Observant
Friars, preaching a strong, Easter sermon against the unlawfulness of his
proposed marriage with Anne. If, like Ahab, he did evil in the sight of
the Lord, then, perhaps, history would record that the dogs licked up
his blood as they had done Ahab's. The next Sunday Henry fared no

better, for Henry Elston, the warden of the Greenwich convent, retorted with anger and effect when from the pulpit Richard Curwen, a royal chaplain, tried to plead Henry's cause. Henry ordered the arrest of Peto and Elston, but that did not silence criticism. Chapuys reported to Charles V that fear of provoking demonstrations against Anne had led Henry to abandon his usual midsummer hunting expedition into the counties north of the Thames. Opposition could make Henry very stubborn, and evidence of Anne's widespread unpopularity did not cause him to waver. On 23 August 1532 the aged Warham died. Henry, emboldened by Cromwell, accepted this as a signal to launch the final attack.

Before Mass on Sunday, 1 September, at Windsor, the countesses of Sussex and Rutland led the Lady Anne through an avenue of courtiers in procession to the throne. Anne knelt before the king, and the bishop of Winchester proclaimed two patents. The first created her marchioness of Pembroke in her own right, and, after her death, granted the title to her eldest son legitimate or illegitimate. The second settled upon her lands worth £1000 a year. Then Henry took from Lady Mary Howard's hands a coronet and a crimson-velvet mantle and placed them on Anne's head and shoulders. This brief, unusual ceremony constituted both the insurance required by Anne before she yielded at last to Henry's importunity and became his mistress, and a defiant determination on Henry's part that his court and people were going to accept his new wife-to-be whatever their private opinions. A month later he sent Norfolk to bid Catherine surrender her jewels so that Anne could wear them, and he busied himself negotiating with Francis for a summit meeting at which Anne could be present. Francis felt there was no need for such a meeting. He remembered 1520 with all its extravagance and lack of lasting results. But he was prepared to humour the insistent Henry on the understanding that it should be a simple meeting and nothing like the ruinous Field of the Cloth of Gold. Henry wanted the meeting chiefly so that Anne could receive official French recognition, and soon after 1 September he informed several noblemen that their wives would be required to accompany the marchioness to Calais. The bigger difficulty was for Francis to find a French lady suitable to receive Anne. Clearly Queen Eleanor, a niece of Catherine, would not do. Marguerite, the king's sister, refused, and Henry would not agree that Anne should be welcomed by the duchess of Vendôme, whom both courts associated with a number of well-known scandals. In the end Henry had to accept that Anne should not accompany him to the actual meeting. But she rode with him through Kent and crossed to Calais with the main party on 11 October. Ten days later Henry led his court to Boulogne. He could never resist display, and despite his agreement with Francis to cut down expense, his men were lavishly dressed and accoutred to impress the French: for himself Henry chose russet velvet richly covered with gold, pearls, and precious stones. The two kings met at the frontier between Calais and France, and after embracing and exchanging friendly if formal greetings, rode into Boulogne for three days of feasting and merrymaking. By fair words and loose purse-strings Henry set out to ingratiate himself with as many important Frenchmen as he could, and when Francis returned with him to Calais contrived that he should meet Anne. After supper on Sunday, 27 October, eight masked ladies came into the room to dance with the leading guests. When the masks were removed, Francis discovered that his partner had been the new marchioness, but he successfully carried off what might have been an embarrassing situation. Henry took courage and comfort from this meeting with Francis. It had not given Anne the recognition he had hoped for, but Francis had promised to intervene again in Rome and try and arrange a personal meeting with Clement. Henry did not allow past disappointments with the fair words of princes to depress him. When he stepped ashore at Dover on 13 November he confidently anticipated that the plan which Cromwell had put into his mind and which he was already planning in detail would cause no unpleasant consequences overseas.

To replace Warham as archbishop of Canterbury, Henry chose Thomas Cranmer, archdeacon of Taunton. Since the beginning of 1532 Cranmer had been Henry's ambassador at the Imperial court. Consequently news of his elevation had to pursue him on the Continent and did not reach him until mid-November. After that everything was bustle and haste. Normally the crown kept a see vacant for at least several months in order to enjoy its revenues, but this time Henry required the services of the new archbishop even more than Canterbury's rents and fees. By Christmas Cranmer was back in England, and Henry had found him money so that he could make immediate application in Rome for the bulls confirming his appointment. Neither the emperor nor the papal nuncio, whom Henry took care to flatter, objected to Cranmer becoming archbishop, and two French cardinals, one de Grammont, timely present in Rome on behalf of Francis I, asked Clement to acquiesce. The warning dispatches which Chapuys sent to Charles were discredited by arguments that Henry had given Anne the marquisate as compensation and not as preparation for the queen's throne. It pleased Clement to grant Henry this apparently harmless request after having been compelled to refuse him so much, and early in March 1533 he sealed the formal papers in Rome. On 30 March Cranmer was consecrated archbishop.

Henry could hardly believe his good fortune. Had Clement refused or even delayed to confirm Cranmer's appointment, he would have placed Henry in a desperate position. As it was, it was a close enough shave, for in January Anne had realised she was pregnant. So that her child, the long-awaited son and heir according to Henry, could be free from all suggestion of illegitimacy, Henry had secretly married Anne on or about 25 January, the feast of the Conversion of St. Paul. If Cranmer's application in Rome was to have any chance of success, absolute secrecy was essential. So completely was the secret kept that it has never been possible to say with certainty where, by whom, or before what witnesses the ceremony was performed, although circumstantial evidence suggests that it probably took place either at Greenwich or York House in the presence of a handful of Anne's closest relations and friends, and that the officiating priest was George Brown, an Augustinian friar, well-known for his support of Henry's point of view.

Henceforward time became the most important factor. A careless word or gesture could inform the world; in particular, Anne's pregnancy could not be kept secret much longer, and, if the heir was to be legally recognised, it would be politic for pregnancy and marriage to become public together. Parliament assembled on 4 February. Henry appeared at the opening ceremony flanked on one side by the French ambassador and on the other by the papal nuncio. He intended that their presence, unusual and therefore provocative of comment, should give lords and commons the impression that what he asked of this session had the approval of his ally Francis, and of the pope himself. He revealed his plans in a government bill as soon as he felt Cranmer's nomination safe. As usual the preamble set out the justification for the new law. England was and always had been an 'empire', a complete unit, 'governed by one Supreme Head and King . . . unto whom a body politic, compact of all sorts and degrees of people divided in terms by names of Spirituality and Temporalty, be bounden and owe to bear next to God a natural and humble obedience'. Under the king, the English church was 'meet of itself, without the intermeddling of any exterior person or persons'. Kings Edward I, Edward II, Richard II, Henry IV and others had put their seal on various laws to protect England 'from the annoyance as well of the see of Rome as from the authority of other foreign potentates', but these laws had proved insufficient for they did not cover 'causes testamentary, causes of matrimony and divorces, rights of tithes, oblations, and obventions'. Therefore in his new bill Henry proposed that all such cases should henceforward be adjudged and finally determined not at Rome but within the realm of England. From an archdeacon's decision appeal could be made to a bishop, and from a bishop's decision to the final judgment of the archbishop, or, in causes touching the crown, to the upper house of convocation. But no appeals whatsoever could henceforward be made to the pope.

The bill, admirably and patiently contrived, appealed to nationalistic feeling, and did everything possible to disguise its true purpose. Cromwell arranged considerable lobbying of members of both houses, but yet the bill encountered a core of resistance in the commons. Many members did not wish to vote extra authority to bishops, and those whose thoughts centred on trade with the Netherlands feared that the bill might provoke Charles to exact economic sanctions. But within a fortnight government spokesmen overrode the opposition, and the commons passed the bill. Simultaneously convocation was discussing the motion that no pope by dispensation could sanction marriage with a brother's widow. Stokesley of London presided and pushed the motion through a depleted house, so that by the time Cranmer had been consecrated archbishop and granted the authority of *legatus natus* of the Holy See, the legal barriers which had obstructed his predetermined course had been broken down.

It no longer mattered that Anne's marriage should be kept secret. Henry told council about it, and on 9 April sent Norfolk and others to Catherine to require her voluntarily to surrender her title as queen and assume the title of princess dowager. Catherine naturally refused to do so, and compelled Norfolk to tell her the brutal truth that Henry had married Anne more than two months ago. Next day the news spread rapidly through the court, and on 12 April Anne openly assumed her place as queen. Even the duchesses had no option but to bow the knee before the daughter of the man they still thought of as Sir Thomas Boleyn.

The Coronation of Queen Anne

Most men and women outside London first heard of the new queen when their parish priest prayed for the well-being of 'Henry and Anne' instead of the familiar 'Henry and Catherine'. Councillors and courtiers kept abreast of the king's affairs, but outside the court, and still more outside London, few people knew how fast events were moving. The sudden realisation of the position evoked a wave of sympathy for Catherine and contempt for Anne, which Henry could only ignore in the hope that it would soon die down. Meantime, he and Cranmer continued to complete the legal formalities. The end was never in doubt, but for the sake of the record and good appearances, procedure had to go forward at a dignified and stately pace. It might be only a charade, but Henry required it to be an elaborate, fully dressed pro-duction.

On 11 April Cranmer wrote to Henry asking if he could have gracious permission to examine and finally determine the king's 'great cause of matrimony' in order that he could exonerate his conscience towards God and satisfy his bounden duty towards his king. Henry replied at great length. He demonstrated how correct Cranmer was to petition humbly, for 'God and we' ordained him primate 'to order, judge, and determine mere spiritual causes within our realm': 'you cannot enterprise any part of your said office in so weighty and great a cause pertaining to us, being your prince and sovereign, without our licence obtained so to do'. Nevertheless, although Henry recognised no superior and was not 'subject to the laws of any earthly creature', he would not refuse Cranmer's humble request 'to make an end, according to the will and pleasure of Almighty God, in our said great cause of matrimony'. Armed with this royal rigmarole, Cranmer summoned his court to the Augustinian priory at Dunstable, sufficiently far away to be free from London demonstrators. Already he had served his writ upon Catherine, but neither he nor anyone else expected her to attend. Although she had absolutely refused to associate herself with Eustace Chapuys's appeal to the emperor to declare war on Henry without delay, she was equally determined to give not the slightest recognition to Cranmer's authority. Therefore the court declared her contumacious, and on 9 May sat down to the tedious farce of hearing evidence and counsel. A fortnight later Cranmer considered he could decently pronounce the predetermined verdict that Henry and Catherine had never been legally married because his court had established that Catherine's former marriage to Arthur had been consummated. The new statute of appeals forbade any further questioning of this verdict. Five days later, Cranmer completed Henry's legal justification by announcing that he had investigated the circumstances of his secret marriage with Anne, and was satisfied that the union was valid.

That very day, Thursday 29 May, the mayor of London, Sir Stephen Peacock, led a fleet of fifty gaily-bedecked barges down the Thames to Greenwich, where they 'cast anker makyng great melody' with their trumpets, shawms, sackbuts, and 'dyvers other melodious intrumentes'. At three o'clock Anne, accompanied by her ladies and escorted by bishops and noblemen, walked out of the palace and down the water-stairs, took her place in the queen's barge which flaunted her new, fancifully devised coat-of-arms, and at the head of this riverful of craft sailed upstream to the Tower. All other vessels drew towards the banks, and 'shotte divers peales of gunnes' in salutation of the new queen. At the Tower the lord chamberlain received Anne as she stepped ashore and escorted her to the waiting Henry. Two days later she made her formal entry into London. By the king's orders nothing was neglected. The city authorities freshly gravelled the processional route, and set up barriers to keep back the expected crowds. Henry's officers ensured that a full force of nobles, clerics, and city dignitaries were on parade. Twelve Frenchmen, dressed in blue velvet with sleeves slashed with yellow, led the procession. After them filed in order of precedence gentlemen, squires, knights, judges, abbots, barons, bishops, earls, marquises and the high dignitaries who had special parts to play in the coronation ceremonies. Anne herself rode in a horse-litter of white cloth-of-gold. Aloft over her head four knights carried a rich canopy, and close behind her came her ladies of the court.

The procession made slow progress from the Tower to Temple Bar and thence to Whitehall, because at many street-corners different city guilds and companies of foreign merchants had set up elaborate pageants, all of which Anne had to inspect since they had been contrived, ostensibly at least, in her honour. If some attempted to convey a double meaning, Anne's smile of approval for the more obvious interpretation had to appear to mask her eyes against the discordant detail which upheld Catherine's claim to the throne. No unseemly incident marred the long progress, though some observers perceived little enthusiasm and heard hostile comments and spiteful jests. The following day, Whit Sunday, everyone of consequence saw Anne crowned at Westminster Abbey with full pomp and splendour. The long blue, red, gold, and white procession moved slowly through the west door. Anne, dressed in purple velvet trimmed with ermine, walked up the nave escorted by the bishops of London and Winchester, and followed by her ladies. Cranmer received her in the chancel, and as the ceremony proceeded he 'set the croune of saint Edward on her head, and then delivered her the scepter of gold in her right hand, and the rod of Ivery with the dove in the left hand, and then all the quere sang *Te deum*'. Mass followed, after which everyone moved to Westminster Hall for the coronation feast. In all this pageantry Henry took no part. With unusual self-denial he allowed Anne to be the sole centre of attraction, and contented himself with watching the feast from a hide specially constructed in the newly built cloisters of St. Stephen's. But for the next ten days he and Anne led the court through the inevitable succession of banquets and tournaments first at Westminster and later at Greenwich. Such lavish publicity compensated Anne for the secrecy of her wedding, but it also burned Henry's boats. Whatever consequences his recent actions might entail, he could never easily return to his original position.

Ever since his marriage to Anne had become public knowledge, Henry, with Cromwell at his side, had watched uneasily for reactions in Europe. He expected Clement and Emperor Charles to be angry at what he had done, but he was both surprised and hurt when Francis, who had been encouraging him to go ahead and solve his own problems, denounced the Dunstable court and bewailed Anne's coronation. Francis wanted to keep England at his heel; it would have suited him best if Henry had continued to plead his cause in Rome and look for French support there. But Henry could not entertain such a policy, partly because it would throw doubts upon the legitimacy of the child soon to be born, and partly because he was now prepared to destroy every fragment of papal authority in England if Clement did not quickly approve his new marriage. Henry enjoyed the bravado of his precarious independence. He knew there was danger in his political isolation—even the Lutherans were not likely allies—but under Cromwell's quiet tutelage he confidently looked to internal division and rivalries in Europe to give him sufficient time to consolidate his new position.

When Clement heard of the statute of appeals he spoke angrily of the treachery of both Henry and Francis, and insisted that the papal court should continue its hearing of Henry's matrimonial cause. Henry knew that an adverse verdict in Rome might encourage opposition to the crown in England. He therefore tried to deter Clement by issuing the letters patent necessary to put the act of annates into effect, and in a precautionary attempt to counter possible legal complications later, he registered before the archbishop of York an appeal to a general council of the church, as an authority superior to the papacy. Clement knew nothing of this second move, but he felt he could not afford to ignore Henry's challenge. He would have liked either Charles or Francis or both to become his secular arm and go to war against England. That neither monarch showed any desire to assume this honour did not prevent him on 11 July from publicly condemning Henry's second marriage, and, on pain of excommunication, giving him, Anne, and Cranmer six weeks in which to turn the clock back to before the meeting of the Dunstable court. The English ambassadors at Rome passed this infuriating news to the duke of Norfolk, who was in France trying without much success to improve Anglo-French understanding. Immediately, badly shaken by the report, he sent Rochford, Anne's brother, post-haste to London to ask for further instructions. The news angered Henry and temporarily shook his confidence. On Cromwell's advice, he ordered Norfolk to try once more to keep Francis and Clement apart, recalled his ambassadors from Rome, and, as a desperate insurance against war, sent Stephen Vaughan, one of Cromwell's intimates, to sound the Protestant princes of Germany about the possibilities of an alliance against the emperor. An unsatisfactory audience with King Francis in Montpellier increased Norfolk's pessimism, and at the end of August 1533 Bishop Gardiner replaced him as Henry's ambassador at the French court. His instructions were to prevent the breach in Anglo-French affairs from widening.

During the weeks which followed Anne's coronation, Henry's chief concern was not foreign affairs but his queen's health and the well-being of the child she was carrying. He took care to shield her from bad or alarming news, although when once she remonstrated with him for deserting her for another lady, he could not prevent himself from deflating her jealous indignation by angrily reminding her that he could reduce her status to the dust just as easily as he had raised her to the throne. Not even the mother of his long-awaited son must question his right to do anything he wished. He had no doubt at all that the child was going to be a son. Astrologers and soothsayers earned easy money by telling him so, and the court doctors with all their modern learning agreed that it would be a boy. Indeed, Henry would probably have dealt harshly with anyone who dared to say otherwise. 'God who knows my righteous heart always prospers my affairs', he declared with bland assurance. But when the baby was born at Greenwich on the first Sunday in September, it was a girl. Tears of disappointment clouded Henry's eyes, but later he consoled himself by reasoning that if Anne could bear so healthy a baby girl now, she would probably give him a son next time. Stokesley, bishop of London, christened the baby *Elizabeth* in the church of the Observant Friars at Greenwich. Cranmer stood as godfather. The citizens of London lit bonfires and enjoyed freely flowing wine, but how spontaneous, contrived, or cynical were the popular celebrations for the birth of the future Queen Elizabeth it is impossible to say. Certainly there were mutterings against Anne when Henry inevitably proclaimed Elizabeth princess of Wales and deprived Mary of that title. General sympathy lay as much with Mary as with Catherine, but Henry could hardly go to so much trouble to establish the legality of his marriage to Anne and then refuse to recognise Elizabeth as his heir-presumptive.

Cromwell still had faith that his 'brinkmanship' policy abroad would succeed. He admitted Chapuys's point that active Imperial opposition, even if it fell short of war, would be harmful to Henry, but he also knew that it would damage Charles too. The Flemings would kick against a trade ban quite as hard as the Londoners, and the balance of power in western Europe was too delicately poised for Charles to add one more to his implacable enemies. Nor did Cromwell think that Clement would dare denounce Henry irrevocably. He sometimes wished he would, for it would be easier to rally Englishmen behind the crown if the pope became aggressive and attacked their king. As if to prove Cromwell right, Clement officially postponed sentence on Henry at the end of September. He hoped against hope that his coming meeting with Francis at Marseilles would produce an acceptable compromise. Conversations began on 12 October. Clement rejected Henry's bald demand that he should then and there declare everything settled in Henry's favour, but he offered to transfer the court to Avignon if Henry would only continue to recognise papal authority. This was the crux. Henry had more than half-broken with Rome already, and the surprising lack of ill-consequences had made him prouder and more aggressive than ever. Both Anne and Cromwell were urging him to make the break complete, but whereas Anne was anxious to retain the friendship of France because a *rapprochement* between Henry and Charles promised her no comfort or security, Cromwell was inclined to agree with Chapuys that in the complicated diplomatic situation in Europe, it would pay both Henry and Charles to seek reconciliation. Francis would try and prevent this, for in the north he required English neutrality if not English co-operation. Unfortunately for him, he knew that he would blast his ambitious hopes in Italy if he won Henry's support by opposing Clement.

Henry showed appreciation of this finely balanced diplomacy only by feeling free to demand and threaten. At Marseilles, Gardiner, hamstrung by his instructions that Henry must have Clement's immediate capitulation, could only submit the Avignon offer to London. His courier found Henry still spluttering over the news that Francis had failed to compel the pope to accept his peremptory demand, and consequently the dispatch sent back to Marseilles was adamant. Gardiner was to reject the Avignon proposal as worse than the Cambrai proposal which Henry had turned down earlier, and to threaten to call a general council, 'which will more fear the pope than all other things', if Clement insisted upon being obstinate. In some trepidation Gardiner tested Francis's reactions first. They were not encouraging, for the king denounced Henry's uncompromising attitude, and declared that if his threats led to his being excommunicated, he must not look to France for help. Nevertheless, Gardiner had no option but to obey orders. He broke the news to Clement as gently as he could, but he could not avoid making the pope very angry indeed. Clement dismissed Henry's appeal to a general council as illegal and insulting, but he heeded

French wishes sufficiently to keep the negotiating door slightly
ajar.

Meantime, in London, Henry was not helping Francis nor making
Clement's position any easier. On 9 November, two days after
Gardiner had had his audience with the pope, he shocked Norfolk,
Anne, and the other francophiles at court by turning the official leave-
taking of Jean de Dinteville, the departing French ambassador, into a
tirade against French deception and desertion. Dinteville reported this
incident to Francis, and described it as symptomatic of the new mood
at the English court. Jean du Bellay, bishop of Paris, volunteered to try
and salvage Anglo-French friendship. He arrived in London a week
before Christmas, and found that Henry had everything prepared for
parliament to complete England's breach with Rome. Despite his
friendship with the Boleyns, the bishop's mixture of pleadings and
threats could only persuade Henry to agree to do nothing irretrievable
for the next two months, and even then Henry made it quite plain that
he would require Clement to come right over to his side, publicly
denouncing Catherine and accepting Anne, before he would consider
modifying his policy. A year or two earlier, Henry had watched the
shifts of power in Europe constantly and apprehensively. Now he
showed towards them a majestic indifference. His own and Cromwell's
reasoning had convinced him that he could do what he liked in England;
the bolder he was the less other kings were likely to intervene.

Other People's Consciences

If danger lay anywhere it lay in England itself. Most of the nobles
and leading clergy were papists and opposed to the Boleyn faction. The
city stood firmly by an alliance with the Empire for the sake of trade
with the Low Countries, and the masses, despite their adoration of
Henry, instinctively felt loyalty for Catherine and mistrust for Anne.
In purely religious matters tradition was strongly entrenched. Cromwell
knew this, and Henry must have suspected it. Therefore, careful preparation had to smooth the passage of the final bills through parliament.
The presses turned out pamphlets, preachers delivered favourable sermons, and official letters 'excused' known friends of Catherine from
attending the house of lords. Above all, possible leaders of opposition
had either to be silenced or terrified into inaction. Henry delighted in

popularity, but he refused to tolerate opposition from any quarter or for any reason. His keen nose scented treason where none existed, for he did not distinguish between political opponents and conscientious objectors. Those who were not for him abjectly and whole-heartedly he deemed to be against him and worthy of death. He needed no Cromwell to teach him what to do with political traitors, but Cromwell was even more astute than he was in uncovering and defining treason. He accepted Machiavelli's dictum that desirable though it might be for a prince to be both feared and loved, it was safer for him to be feared if circumstances forced him to choose between the two.

Cromwell used a pathetic nun in Kent to frighten a number of possible opposition leaders. For several years Elizabeth Barton, a member of the community of St. Sepulchre at Canterbury, had enjoyed a reputation as a mystic and prophetess. Her earlier prophecies were trivial or ambiguous, but the respect shown her by several leading ecclesiastics and the excessive attention and flattery paid her by hosts of credulous acquaintances made her bolder. She ventured into politics, and claimed that angels had told her that Henry would meet with disaster if he married Anne, and, later, that they had shown her the place in Hell prepared for him. Henry had first heard of Elizabeth Barton in Warham's day. He had granted her an audience, and had listened to her advice. By 1533, however, Cromwell was able to show him how dangerous this nun might be. The matrimonial problem was now solved: no longer was it, even in theory, a matter of opinion. Yet at least two Canterbury monks, Bocking and Dering, and two Observant friars, Risby and Rich, were spreading the nun's hostile words far and wide. In July Henry ordered Cranmer to examine her, and simple, innocent Elizabeth rewarded the archbishop's gentle approach by pouring out not only treasonable opinions and prophecies, but also the names of dozens of men and women who had listened to her revelations. Cromwell could have desired nothing better. In November 1533 he pounced. He imprisoned Elizabeth in the Tower, and charged with treason a number of clergy and laymen who had been publicising her prophecies. Others, including John Fisher, Thomas More, the marchioness of Exeter, and the countesses of Salisbury and Derby, he ordered to be examined for failing to report a known treason, and before a large gathering of notables, Chancellor Audley seriously maintained that the pope had been induced to act against Henry by the 'damnable and diabolic instrumentality' of the nun. Henry could make what he wished out of the charges. At first he was content that Elizabeth by public confession and denunciation should kill her reputation among the common folk, but he kept her and her closest adherents in gaol ready for possible future uses. Already they had served the commendable purpose of spreading fear and apprehension into many hearts, for Cromwell, though he had hinted that Catherine and Mary were on it, had carefully refrained from publishing a list of suspects.

In such matters of public policy Henry looked to Cromwell for advice, but in his continual harassing of Catherine and Mary he seems to have responded to Anne's constant petulance and pin-pricking, as well as to Cromwell's rational fear that a defiant Catherine might easily become the centre of a conspiracy against the crown. Henry's problem with Catherine and Mary was not unlike that which, a generation later, Elizabeth was to face with Mary Stuart. Personal and political considerations forbade any arbitrary, violent action against them, and yet their very existence endangered the peace of the realm. Chapuys encouraged Catherine in the hope that one day public opinion and foreign pressure might compel Henry to restore her to the throne. In July 1533 Henry ordered that Catherine should be removed from Ampthill in the Bedfordshire countryside to a lonely house at Buckden on the edge of the fens in Huntingdonshire. But this did not hide her away sufficiently. In October Cromwell arrested two Observant friars who were travelling back to Flanders after visiting Catherine. The rack failed to stretch out of them evidence damaging enough to condemn the old queen, but Henry decided that her freedom should be further restricted. Before Christmas he sent Suffolk, the gallant, to Buckden to purge Catherine's household of all who still insisted upon paying her the respects due to a queen, and to remove Catherine either to the strongly fortified castle of Fotheringhay or to Somersham, a house in the Cambridge fens accessible only by a causeway. Suffolk had no success whatever. The servants refused to be intimidated, and Catherine shut herself into her private rooms and defied Suffolk to shift her. In the end the duke had to leave her where she was. He took back to London some furniture and hangings, and he arrested a few servants, but Catherine remained at Buckden. Princess Mary adopted a similar policy. She avoided treasonable utterances—she left it to others to suggest that she might marry Reginald Pole and claim the throne—but she refused to surrender any right or title. Henry was incensed to think that his daughter, now almost 18 years old, should listen so carefully to her mother but not to him. He removed her to Hatfield, baby Elizabeth's new home, but Mary protested that 'the daughter of Lady Pembroke' had no right to the title *princess*. The most she, Mary, was prepared to do was to call Elizabeth *sister*. Lady Shelton, an aunt of Queen Anne, had charge of the two princesses at Hatfield. She was under instructions to keep Mary strictly controlled, but it does not appear that she attempted to subdue her unduly. Indeed Henry himself found it hard to maintain his harsh attitude towards the two women whom he had once loved and admired. He steadfastly refused to sanction using force against Catherine, and in several ways showed that he still thought kindly of Mary. He blustered about wielding the axe against those friends who were encouraging her with false hopes to be wilful, but when he visited Hatfield he paid courtesies to both his daughters, when the French ambassador sang Mary's praises he could not keep the tears out of his eyes, and when, in March 1534, Francis suggested that it would be good tactics if Mary married Duke Alexander of Florence, he thought it outrageous that anyone below royal rank should be proposed as a fit husband for one of his daughters.

The Act of Succession

Henry convened parliament again in January 1534. He had promised du Bellay that he would do nothing irretrievable before the end of February, but he had no intention of upsetting his arranged schedule. If Clement capitulated, policy could always be modified; if, as was more likely, he made insufficient concessions, then steady preparations for the final breach would convince him that Henry was in earnest. The patience which Henry had shown during the complicated negotiations between 1526 and 1531 had all evaporated. He was now an irascible man threatening 'to give such a buffet to the Pope as he never had before'.

The first act of the new session merely put into impeccable legal form what was already general practice. It forbade payment to Rome of any 'sums of money for annates, firstfruits or otherwise for expedition of bulls, briefs, or palls', and decreed that all future bishops and archbishops would be elected by the cathedral chapter accepting without question the king's nominee. The second act deprived the papacy of Peter's pence, a small traditional sum paid by the English church, and arranged that, instead of Rome, Canterbury should henceforward issue 'licences, dispensations, compositions, faculties, grants, rescripts, delegacies, or any other instruments or writings'. A far more significant act modified the restraint of appeals act passed in 1533; by arranging that litigants could appeal from the archbishop's court to the 'King's Majesty in the King's Court of Chancery', it destroyed the independence of the ecclesiastical judicature. A fourth act, the act of succession, confirmed the validity of Henry's marriage to Anne and declared that the crown should pass to their children. Anyone who 'maliciously or obstinately' published or uttered anything 'to the slander or prejudice' of the marriage would be guilty of misprision of treason, and liable to imprisonment and confiscation of all his possessions. Probably many people detested this particular act, but few spoke out against it. Inside the lords and commons, the ministers of the crown, yielding only that the word *maliciously* should be added to the original draft, carried the day. Outside parliament, most of those who disagreed with the contents of the act acknowledged, as Thomas More did, that undoubtedly parliament had the right to fix the succession to the throne.

Henry and his ministers cleverly manœuvred these acts through parliament. They allowed opponents to spend their energy on such unessentials as the phrasing of a declaration that convocation approved Henry's marriage to Anne, on the rejection of a bill to settle a pension on 'the princess dowager', or on the modification of the list of those who should be charged with treason for encouraging the nun of Kent. Very few members of parliament understood the true nature of the revolution they were making. The majority would never have expressed themselves in favour of England cutting herself off from the church of Rome, but they raised no serious objection when the crown took yet another step to that end. With clear consciences they could approve a single measure to put pressure on the pope or to curtail the power of the clergy. Here and there they forced Henry to yield a detail, but only too late did they realise how one act led logically to another, so that the cumulative effect frightened them. They were like a defending army, which, retreating tactically from point to point too long, never finds a line on which to stand and fight.

Continental observers could only see what was happening in England

19 THE PRINCESS MARY
*Detail of an anonymous
portrait, c. 1535*

20 THE PRINCESS
ELIZABETH
*etail of an anony-
ous portrait, c. 1547;
roduced by gracious
rmission of H.M.
The Queen*

21   EDWARD, PRINCE OF WALES

From a chalk and watercolour drawing by Hans Holbein c. 1541

through a thin smoke-screen of diplomacy, which distorted if it did not obscure their view. On his return from London at the end of December 1533, du Bellay had convinced Francis that his only chance of retaining the alliance of both England and Rome was to persuade Clement to act as Henry wished. He flattered himself that he could do this, and, with the approval of his king, went to Rome. Clement led du Bellay to think that he was reconsidering the problem, and in February the bishop wrote an over-favourable report of his progress to Castillon, the French ambassador in London. Henry encouraged French hopes of a settlement, but by mid-March Castillon knew that he would accept from Rome nothing but immediate and final judgment in his favour. Clement was equally firm-minded. While parliament was completing the legal process of separation, the consistory court in Rome was steadily moving to its decision. At length, on 23 March, the very day the lords were giving a third reading to the bill of succession, the Roman court delivered its long-considered verdict and decreed that Henry and Catherine had been validly married.

Henry and Clement were each satisfied that he had acted according to the will of God, but Henry was not content with success. He wanted victory too. Consequently, he issued instructions that men and women prominent in every sphere of national life, should be required to confirm the act of succession by oath. This implied declaring that papal jurisdiction no longer ran in England, so that opponents of the breach with Rome could not now avoid either surrendering or openly defying the new statutes. Henry showed no respect for conscience, habit, or rank when he encountered opposition. Those who persisted in denouncing his second marriage or opposing his supremacy in the church—and he hardly distinguished between the two—he regarded not as martyrs for their cause, but as traitors to their king. They well deserved their execution—and torture if need be—and their suffering would serve as a warning to others who might be scheming against the crown. On 12 April 1534 the hangman carried out at Tyburn the act which condemned the nun of Kent and four of her closest friends to the barbarities of a traitor's death. The lords had insisted upon removing More's name from the bill, but he sized up the situation exactly when he said that the trouble had been deferred and not removed. For the next 18 months Henry's commissioners relentlessly pursued every known opponent. In the hunt the king showed more determination than any of his ministers and more ruthlessness than Cromwell. To him there was no possible alternative to full submission except the scaffold. The friars were Henry's first quarry because, as itinerant preachers, they had so wide an influence. Only the Observants resisted, and the king quickly and effectively dealt with them by imprisoning a number in the Tower, loading others with chains in monasteries or castles, and forcing the rest to flee abroad. He did not hesitate to use torture and threaten the noose against the members of this, his one-time favourite order. By the end of August 1534 the 200 English Observants had been rendered harmless, and their seven houses closed. During the second half of 1534 royal commissioners administered the oath of succession to monastic communities throughout England and Wales. Only the nine Carthusian houses and the Bridgettine community at Syon refused to take the corporate oath accepting the act and denying the authority of 'the bishop of Rome' in England. For the moment Henry was prepared to leave the Carthusians and Bridgettines in their cells: they could not damage his authority as the Observants could. But when parliament met again in November 1534 he required it to define the new law even more meticulously by passing the act of supremacy and the treason act. The first left not a shadow of doubt that 'the King's Majesty justly and rightfully is and ought to be the Supreme Head of the Church of England': the second catalogued the different forms of treason and declared that 'none offender in any kinds of high treasons . . . shall be admitted to have the benefit or privilege of any manner of sanctuary'.

Henry did not need these new legal weapons to defeat the few resolute men who still opposed his will, but they made him feel more terrifying and look more justified. He renewed his campaign by arresting Carthusian and Bridgettine leaders, bringing them before a secular tribunal, and having them condemned by jury. On 4 May 1535 Richard Reynolds, a scholarly priest at Syon, and the priors of the Charterhouses at London, Beauvale in Nottinghamshire, and Axholme in Lincolnshire were dragged to Tyburn, and, along with John Hale, the elderly vicar of Isleworth, were one by one hanged, drawn, and quartered. A day or two later three other leaders of the London Charterhouse, including Sebastian Newdigate, an old personal friend of Henry, were taken to Marshalsea prison and subjected to a fortnight's hideous torture. Afterwards they were charged with treason, and when they still refused to yield, in the very month that 14 Anabaptists were burned at English stakes for preaching Protestant heresies, they suffered the same fate as the priors. From this moment onwards Henry subjected Syon and the London Charterhouse to continuous pressure. To suppress either outright he believed would be too dangerous, for in an England in which most laymen condemned the majority of religious as privileged drones, these two communities stood out as high-principled, zealous, and sincere. By the end of the year Henry was satisfied with the submission Syon finally offered, but the Carthusians continued to resist until Henry, outraged beyond words by their defiance, overrode Cromwell's more cautious policy. From some he finally wrung a despairing oath, but the ten who remained 'unmoved, unshaken, unseduced, unterrified' he simply chained up in Newgate prison in May 1537 and left to die.

John Fisher and Thomas More had no religious community to give them comfort and strength in their single combat against Henry's will. Fisher admitted that he had said that the king could not possibly be supreme head on earth of the church of England, but he claimed that he had spoken in confidence and without malice. The judge swept aside his plea that the statute of treason condemned only those who *maliciously* questioned the king's title, and on 22 June 1535 the ailing, ascetic bishop suffered beheading at Tyburn. Earlier in his life Thomas More had been an ardent hunter of heretics, but in his last years he showed no 'intention to meddle' with other men's consciences. He had no desire to be a martyr for any cause, but his legal mind could not accept that England, 'being but one poor member in respect of the whole', could make a valid law against the universal church. When More had been chancellor, Henry had not pressed him to support his marriage to Anne, but now king and political situation had both changed. Henry could tolerate no dissension whatever, and on 6 July, More, confessing himself to be 'the king's good servant, but God's first', followed Fisher to the block. This heartless destruction of eminent men shocked scholars and churchmen throughout Europe, but to Henry himself ridding England of a handful of stubborn, misled zealots seemed a comparatively minor matter. Had they not insisted upon setting their prejudices above the collective wisdom of parliament, they could have been a powerful help instead of a stubborn hindrance to their king and his cause. They had preferred to listen to a foreign power. Reynolds had been so deluded as to declare at his trial that 'all good men' in their hearts opposed the king's policy, when nothing was clearer to see than that this very policy had given Englishmen pride in their country's newly found independence. Lords, commons, and even convocation had confirmed each stage of this striking achievement. A few individualists could not be allowed to jeopardise so much good. Everyone must show their loyalty by taking the oath of succession, or suffer the consequences.

HENRY IN STATE
From a Wolsey patent, 1530

5 THE BLOCK AND THE GALLOWS

You will save me all unnecessary pain by taking off my head in one stroke.
Reported last words of THOMAS CROMWELL

Everyone included Catherine and Mary. With them Henry had much more cause for concern. Not only were his personal feelings more closely involved, but also a policy which merely looked severe might push the emperor into declaring war on England, or provoke English sympathisers to rebel. On the other hand neither Henry's temperament nor his prestige could tolerate the ladies' defiance indefinitely. When Catherine refused to take the oath in May 1534, Henry ordered her removal from Buckden to Kimbolton, a stronger and gloomier house. He nominated Sir Edmund Bedingfield and Sir Edward Chamberlain, two reliable servants, to guard and watch her, yet remarkably she kept in touch with Chapuys, who was playing the dangerous game of sounding English acquaintances about their willingness to revolt in Catherine's favour. He wrote to Charles V that he believed the widespread disquiet he had found in England could be easily transformed into successful rebellion. Many noblemen and gentlemen detested Cromwell as they had once hated Wolsey, London was as nervous as ever about the safety of her trade with the Netherlands, and thousands of villagers were blaming increasing taxation, enclosure difficulties, and even the bad weather and ruinous harvest of 1535 on Henry's sinful putting away of the old queen. But this combustible material needed firing, and only two people could do it. The pope might possibly ignite it by publishing Henry's excommunication and calling on all loyal sons of the church to depose him, but a surer way of causing it to blaze quickly would be for Catherine to appeal to Englishmen to redress her wrongs. Hope and desire directed Chapuys's reasoning, yet

Henry too realised the danger. He told his council that if Catherine took it into her head, she could wage as fierce a war against him as ever her mother, Isabella, had fought in Spain. Fortunately for Henry and for England, Catherine loathed the thought of being the cause of bloodshed and suffering.

Henry faced an even more difficult problem with Mary. Despite humiliations and threats, his daughter stubbornly and in his opinion ungratefully, refused to take an oath which dishonoured her mother and declared herself a bastard. Henry sent away all her friends and devoted servants, and Mary began to fear that someone in her hostile household would one day use poison to solve her father's dilemma. Chapuys blamed 'the concubine' for Mary's desperate position. He explained to the emperor, 'The King himself is not ill-natured; it is this Anne who has put him in this perverse and wicked temper and alienates him from his former humanity'. But when, in the spring of 1535, tension and unkindness made Mary seriously ill, Henry's heart softened sufficiently for him to send Dr. Butts to treat her and to allow Catherine's Spanish physician to be called into consultation. He refused, however, to allow Catherine to nurse Mary through her illness. Each of them was explosive enough by herself; together they might blow his kingdom apart.

Anne too had good reason to fear the passive hostility of Catherine and Mary. She was not enjoying the expected fruits of her triumph, because she knew she no longer infatuated her husband. He was making love to at least one other lady at court, and, more serious still, she herself was not again with child. In January 1534, she had announced that she was pregnant, but it had proved a false diagnosis. Six months later Henry had pleaded his wife's pregnancy as an excuse for not crossing the Channel to meet Francis, but at the end of September, after he and Anne had made an extensive progress through the midlands, court gossip was explaining the obvious coolness between them, together with Henry's renewed attentions to the unknown lady, by the fact that the queen had either had a miscarriage or had discovered she was not pregnant after all.

Anne had very few friends in England, and none at all on the Continent. When Clement VII had died at the end of September 1534, the cardinals had elected Alexander Farnese, an anti-imperialist, as the new pope, Paul III. Francis immediately saw possibilities of re-establishing good relations between England and Rome. In November he officially resuscitated the Anglo-French treaty made in London in the far away days of October 1518, and innocently requested that the marriage then arranged between Princess Mary and his eldest son should now take place. It was a clever move, especially as the threatened alternative was for the dauphin to marry Charles V's daughter, Isabella, but it did not trap Henry. He refused the tempting bait, and counter-proposed that if Francis would persuade Paul III to declare Clement's verdict void, he would be willing both to discuss renouncing his title of *King of France*, and to negotiate a marriage between his daughter, Elizabeth, and the dauphin's brother, the duke of Angoulême. He stood firmly by the hard-won act of succession, and both Anne and Cromwell, whose authority and very lives were packaged with the revolution, breathed again. At the same time Henry made reconciliation with Rome more difficult both by announcing his new style, in which the papal *defender of the faith* stood incongruously alongside *on earth supreme head of the English church*, and by bestowing the bishoprics of Salisbury and Worcester on two mild reformers, Nicholas Shaxton and Hugh Latimer. Anne approved of these appointments, but she could not rouse in Henry any sympathy for doctrinal or liturgical reform. He still ordered the execution of heretics, and the burning of reformist books and English translations of the Bible.

During the first half of 1535 Henry and Cromwell sparred rather than negotiated with the French ambassadors. At times they seemed hardly to be discussing the same problems, because Henry's chief concern was to encourage Francis to be tougher with the pope and be prepared to break with Rome if need be, and the ambassadors' instructions were to win England as an active ally against the Empire. Yet both wished to give outsiders the impression that their friendship was firmer than ever. It did not further that end, however, when Paul III raised the imprisoned and condemned Fisher to the rank of cardinal, and persuaded Francis to write a personal letter to Henry pleading for his release. This censorious intervention in what he considered to be a purely domestic matter stung Henry into violent anger. He is reported to have sworn that he would send Fisher's severed head to Rome so that the pope could fit on it the new red hat.

But in truth during these crowded months Henry gave comparatively little thought to foreign affairs. The unfriendly reception English merchants were receiving in many Continental ports seemed of small consequence compared with Anne's new pregnancy, and threats of invasion from across the Channel frightened him less than the plague which had returned to London that wet summer. He stayed longer than usual out of his capital hunting and merry-making. Probably during these holiday months which he spent chiefly in the western counties, Henry first noticed Jane, the pale, demure daughter of Sir John Seymour of Wolf Hall, in Wiltshire. Certainly in the autumn, when a French embassy travelled to Hampshire to meet him, the ambassadors reported that the king was in love again. It was hardly so simple as that, for at the same time as Jane was filling his mind more and more with her quiet charm and gently repulsing his more vigorous advances, Anne was reviving his hopes of a son, and the stubborness of Catherine and Mary was continuing to exasperate him. To make life more difficult, the colder weather did not clear the plague quickly from London, and news arrived that Francis was seriously ill. Francis was not an ideal ally—indeed his latest threat was that he would do just what the pope requested if Henry did not quickly make his peace with Rome—but Henry had no wish to lose him. He believed him to be a powerful brake on papal and Imperial impetuosity, and a brake was never more needed. In July 1535, goaded by news of the execution of Fisher and More, Paul III had warned Catholic princes to be ready to make war on Henry when he called on them to do so. Since then Charles V had returned from a triumphant expedition against Turkish-supported corsairs in Tunis, and was probably freer and more confident than he had ever been to lead a punitive army against England. Henry knew that Catherine's and Mary's resistance encouraged would-be invaders, and Chapuys reported that Henry had vowed that he would soon remove that danger. If the ladies persisted in their obstinacy, the next parliament must attaint them. Chapuys was repeating gossip which he knew would be greedily devoured at the Imperial court, and, even if Henry said this, he may have intended that his words should do no more than threaten. As it worked out circumstances changed so rapidly that his real intention was never put to the test.

Henry would have had no need for an act of attainder had he but caught a glimpse of the letter Catherine wrote to Pope Paul on 15 October 1535. The address alone broke the statute of appeals; the contents, which invited foreign intervention in England, could not

22 THOMAS CROMWELL,
EARL OF ESSEX
*Detail of a portrait after
Hans Holbein*

23 THOMAS CRANMER
*Detail of a portrait by
G. Flicke, 1546*

24   HENRY VIII AND PRINCE EDWARD
From a contemporary cameo; reproduced by gracious permission of H.M. The Queen

25   HENRY VIII
From a lead medal by Hans Schwartz

help but be treason by any law. 'Your Holiness knows, and all Christendom knows, what things are done in England, what great offence is given to God, what scandal to the world, what reproach is thrown upon your Holiness. If a remedy be not applied shortly, there will be no end to ruined souls and martyred saints.' This political bomb, together with covering letters to the emperor and the Imperial ambassador in Rome, Chapuys sent off post-haste. For months he had been beseeching Catherine to make this appeal, and now when at last she had yielded, two sudden deaths foiled his plans. Before Chapuys's courier could reach Rome, the unexpected death of the childless Francesco Sforza opened the way for Francis to renew his claim on Milan, and before there was a chance to see if this claim would end the truce between France and the Empire, Catherine herself died. She became acutely ill in November and died on 7 January 1536. To the end she remained in control of her wits and her affairs. Chapuys saw her two or three days before she died, but Henry made no attempt to visit her nor did he allow Mary to go to Kimbolton. On her last morning, Catherine dictated a letter to Henry forgiving him for the way 'you have cast me into many calamities and yourself into many troubles'. She commended their daughter into his care, and in a final sentence avowed that she longed to see him—'mine eyes desire you above all things. Farewell'. This demonstration of personal affection, however, did not touch Henry's heart: perhaps he could not take his eyes off the defiant signature, *Katherine, Queen of England*. He did not pretend that he was not glad she was dead. 'God be praised,' he shouted, 'we are free from all suspicion of war.' Both Henry and Anne defiantly wore yellow in the last of the Christmastide festivities at Greenwich, for they were not mourning the death of a queen, but celebrating unexpected release, the one from a nagging fear that the emperor might still try to set his aunt free, the other from the silent opposition of a woman she was never allowed to forget for long.

The End of Anne Boleyn

Henry was now in his forty-fifth year. He was still a fine looking man, and appeared to be still enjoying robust health and delighting in his exceptional athletic skill. Four years earlier Lodovico Falier, the Venetian, in a confidential dispatch, had described him as having 'a very well proportioned body of tall stature', and possessing an 'air of royal majesty such as has not been witnessed in any other sovereign for many years'. On a later occasion, he had praised his dexterity and untiring zeal for all sports. But Henry had not escaped the touch of time's finger. Since 1527 he had been troubled by an ulcer on his thigh. He tried to ignore it, but periodically, to his petulant anger, it would break out again. He suffered too from bouts of feverish head-aches and nervous depression. He hardly admitted these changes to himself. Like most active men he was a bad patient, and he strove to maintain his public image of jovial, choleric, bluff King Harry by continuing to dance, hunt, and joust just as enthusiastically as ever. At Greenwich on 17 January, ten days after Catherine's death, he fell so heavily in the lists that he lay unconscious for two hours. Pride pre-vented him from giving himself a decent chance to recover. He refused to acknowledge that Henry Tudor could be seriously damaged merely by being unhorsed, and he struggled to live his usual active life. But gradually his shaken, stiffening body and his ulcerated leg forced him to realise that he could no longer compete with young men. By August he was prepared to whisper in Chapuys's ear that he was beginning to feel old.

Five days after Henry fell so hard on the tilt-yard earth, Anne mis-carried again. The foetus was far enough developed to be declared male: once more Henry had been cheated of his long-wanted son. Anne blamed her miscarriage upon the shock Henry's accident had given her, but Henry, made more dogmatic by his love of Jane Seymour, believed she would never bear him a son. His previous relations with Mary Boleyn had probably incurred divine wrath after all. He now looked at Anne through eyes freed from desire, and asked himself how he had ever come to marry her. The only answer he could seriously accept was that she had bewitched him. He did not try and hide his new contempt of her, so that weeks before Easter many people at home and abroad were speculating about whom he would marry next. Emperor Charles feared he might choose a French princess, but opinion at the English court generally favoured the chances of the quiet mouse, Jane. Regret-tably Anne still lived.

The king's scowl was the signal for councillors and courtiers to take courage and speak and act against the queen. Her unhappy position did not arouse the widespread sympathy which had been offered to

Catherine. She had never been popular: either she had been considered an upstart and an adventuress, or a barrier in the way of a profitable alliance with the Empire. Cromwell and Chapuys thought this a good opportunity to restore good relations between Henry and Charles. Cromwell had little difficulty in weaning most of his fellow councillors from the hope or desire of a French alliance, and Charles sent Chapuys an authority to open negotiations. But Anne had no intention of going down without a struggle. She believed her future well-being depended upon the continuance of the Anglo-French understanding, and since Henry had recovered sufficiently from his angry disappointment over the miscarriage to tolerate her company again, she used all her waning influence to safeguard her interests. At Greenwich on the Tuesday after Easter, Henry granted Chapuys an audience so that he could hear the emperor's latest proposals, but he shocked everyone by his hostile, abusive reception. He cursed both Cromwell and Chapuys as fools, ranted against the emperor's treachery and ingratitude for the friendship he had formerly shown him, and declared that he was on the side of France in the current disputes over Milan and Burgundy. This unexpected outburst frightened Cromwell more than Chapuys, for he always knew that his authority would last only so long as Henry accepted the advice he offered. Under cover of a diplomatic indisposition, he stayed at home for a few days to consider how he might best recover Henry's confidence. He decided that he was too heavily committed to an Imperial alliance to reverse his policy, and that his only hope of retaining power was to remove Anne, destroy the shrinking Boleyn faction, and make it possible for Henry to find happiness and new hopes of an heir in marriage with Jane Seymour. Desperation so spurred him on that he put his plans into effect with extraordinary speed.

Cromwell built his scheme on two reliable foundations—Henry's excessive fear of treason, and Anne's well-known love of male flattery. On 24 April he persuaded the king to commission Audley, Norfolk, Suffolk, Wiltshire, himself and others to hold extraordinary courts to examine suspected traitors and reports of treason. A week later he invited to dinner Mark Smeaton, a young, good-looking groom of the chamber and an elegant dancer, but instead of seating his guest at table, he had him threatened and tortured until he confessed first that he had received money from the queen, and then that he, along with others, had had sexual intercourse with her. This startling news a gratified Cromwell sent to Henry at Greenwich, where the court was holding jousts to celebrate May Day. Without a word to Anne, with whom he had watched the day's sport, Henry left Greenwich that evening, and rode to Westminster. Already he spoke and acted as if Anne's guilt were beyond question, and was full of self-pity for the way he had been deceived. Events moved quickly. Sir Henry Norris, keeper of the privy purse and one of Henry's favourite companions, was arrested on the evidence of Smeaton's confession. He steadfastly denied the charge, but the authorities ignored his protestations and the next day arrested Anne and charged her with committing adultery with Smeaton and Norris. That afternoon she sailed from Greenwich to the Tower in the royal barge. She attracted the attention of the crowds, but she travelled not in great state as she had done three years earlier, but under duress and in disgrace. This time she entered the Tower by Traitors' Gate, and though she was lodged in comfortable apartments, she was continuously watched and denied the consolation of friends. Her gaolers wrote down her distracted and hysterical chatter, so that some of it, suitably interpreted, could be quoted as evidence against her. Her brother, George, Lord Rochford, was seized in Whitehall on the day Anne was made prisoner at Greenwich, and two days later, four other men, Sir Francis Weston, William Brereton, Thomas Wyatt, and Sir Richard Page, were arrested as lovers of the queen. Hardly a soul dared refrain from assuming they were guilty. 'I am clean amazed,' wrote Cranmer, a relatively favourable commentator, 'for I never had better opinion of woman, but I think Your Highness would not have gone so far if she had not been culpable. . . .' The displeasure of the king was death indeed!

No one could complain that the action of the drama dragged, but the course of the plot was clear to all before the first act was over. The charges against Wyatt and Page were dropped, but on 10 and 11 May grand juries found true bills against Smeaton, Norris, Weston, Brereton, and Rochford. All five, even Rochford, were accused of adultery with the queen. In Westminster Hall on 12 May another jury, containing a majority of royal officials, found Smeaton, Norris, Weston, and Brereton guilty, and the judges condemned them to be hanged, drawn and quartered. The queen and her brother faced a court of 26 peers which met in the Tower under the presidency of Norfolk, their uncle. Considerately, Henry did not invite their father, who raised not a finger to help them, to sit on the bench. The prosecution had plenty of evidence, but it was far too nebulous and irrelevant to convince a neutral judge. But no judge or juryman dared to be neutral. On 17 May the five men, spared the tortures of a traitor's death, were beheaded on Tower Green, and two days later the French executioner, specially summoned from Calais, severed Anne's slender neck with his two-handed sword. The cruel, frightening farce was over. Henry had fulfilled his boast that he could degrade Anne as easily as he had raised her to the throne.

The Northern Rising

Henry never saw Anne again after he had ridden from Greenwich so hastily on the evening of May Day 1536. He left it to his ministers to arrange and supervise the progressive stages of arrest, trial, and execution, while he spent those fine spring days merry-making in and around London. After Anne's last miscarriage, Jane Seymour and her brother, Edward, had discreetly withdrawn from court to their family home in Wiltshire, but when Anne was imprisoned in the Tower, they returned to London and were constantly in Henry's company. On several evenings their lamp-lit barge sailed festively by the Tower's dark turrets. They moved to Hampton Court after Anne had been condemned to death, and there Henry joined them once he had arranged for Cranmer to visit the doomed queen and, on the strength of what she told him, declare their marriage invalid. During the days of her imprisonment and trial Henry deliberately demonstrated his indifference to Anne's fate. His final insult came too late to harm Anne herself, but it caused her to die knowing that the law would no longer recognise her daughter as heir to the throne. Anne's execution affected Henry as little as Catherine's death had done. On the following day he and Jane were betrothed at Hampton Court, and ten days later Cranmer married them privately in the queen's apartments at York House.

This sudden transformation—Queen Jane for Queen Anne and all within a month—alarmed Mary and her well-wishers. However odious Anne's offences could be made to appear, no one could seriously maintain that they had threatened the safety of the throne. But Mary's obstinate refusal to take the oaths of succession and supremacy provided a rallying point for all Henry's potential enemies, English and foreign alike. Chapuys and others foresaw that events might begin to run rapidly against Mary as they had recently run against Anne, and they urged her to seek a reconciliation with her father. On 26 May she agreed to ask Cromwell to intercede for her. Henry's immediate reaction was to smile with pleasure for he had never ceased to be fond of her, but when he remembered what her resistance symbolised, he insisted upon full submission to his demands. It took many days of persuasive argument by Chapuys, who believed England would accept her as queen after Henry's death, and of straight-talking and threats from Cromwell, who sought to protect her life, before Mary eventually signed the oaths. After that Henry insisted that she suffered the further humiliation of repeating her submission in the presence of the council. But Jane, whose preference for the traditional in religion gave her great sympathy for Mary, helped her to return to court life. By 8 July Chapuys reported that Mary's treatment was improving every day. All she lacked was the title of princess, 'and that is of no consequence'. In the autumn she lived again at Richmond Palace, and at Christmastide she received handsome gifts from Henry, Jane, and Cromwell. She was almost back into the full court routine, but in her heart she had not changed her beliefs at all.

Before these dramatic events had taken place at court and in the Tower, lords and commons had been meeting at Westminster throughout February, March, and the first half of April 1536. In a busy ten weeks they had at length passed the statute of uses for which Henry had been pressing so long, had tidied up the law concerning tithes, and had made some attempt to solve the chronic problems of vagrancy and enclosures. But the act for which this last session of the Reformation Parliament is best remembered is the one which suppressed monasteries with incomes of less than £200 a year, and transferred their lands and other material possessions to the crown. The 700 or so monasteries and nunneries in England and Wales, together with the 200 friaries, had been doomed ever since parliament had declared Henry to be head of the church in England. All but the Gilbertines were members of orders which had houses in other parts of Christendom. All claimed freedom from the jurisdiction of the local bishop, and though the degree of independence enjoyed by each house differed according to the order it belonged to, it was clear that their conflicting loyalties to pope and king could not long remain indeterminate. Not many people appeared to see this in 1534—abbots and priors cheerfully took the oath of succession—but before the end of 1535 some measure of dissolution was widely anticipated.

In the closing months of 1534 parliament had reimposed the 'intolerable burden' of annates, and had added to it an annual charge of one-tenth of the income of all benefices. These new church taxes, of course, were to be paid to the crown, but before they could be assessed it was necessary to have an up-to-date survey of all ecclesiastical incomes. Cromwell arranged for commissioners to visit each shire, and during the first half of 1535 they revealed to Henry and his ministers the unexpected extent of monastic wealth. In August of the same year Cromwell sent out new commissioners, *visitors*, to bring back evidence to justify an attack on the monasteries. By using a strict interpretation of the monastic rule as their measuring rod, the visitors easily uncovered evidence of widespread slackness and corruption. They high-lighted scandals and abuses in their reports, and quoted names and examples to justify their general, adverse judgments. Cromwell was probably drafting the bill of dissolution while the visitors were still at work, and in March 1536, certainly before there had been adequate time to digest their reports, Henry placed the final text before parliament. In its preamble the bill maintained that though 'in divers and great solemn monasteries' religion 'is right well kept and observed', the visitors had found 'manifest sin, vicious, carnal, and abominable living' in the smaller houses. For the dividing line between vice and virtue Cromwell chose an annual income of £200. This condemned just under half the houses, but brought to the crown no more than £20,000 a year, a mere sixth or seventh of the total monastic wealth. Parliament accepted the bill, and during the spring and summer of 1536 royal officers visited the smaller monasteries, passed over lands, valuables, and debts to the court of augmentations which parliament had created to look after this new royal capital, and either sent the monks to one of the bigger houses, or, theoretically at least, found them a vicarage or pension. At the same time some ambitious or grasping laymen were already making offers and trying to stake their claim for monastic lands which they particularly coveted.

Henry had need for a new act of succession, for thanks to 'the great and intolerable perils and occasions' he was said to have recently 'suffered and sustained', the act of 1534 had lapsed. In June 1536 a newly elected parliament declared that his marriage with Anne was 'of no force, strength, virtue, nor effect'. Therefore, Elizabeth was dismissed with Mary and Henry Fitzroy from the succession, and the crown was entailed first on any sons Henry and Jane might have, secondly on any sons Henry might have by a future wife, and thirdly on Jane's daughters or any other daughters Henry might legitimately father. None of these heirs lived, nor might ever live. So lords and commons, however much they might 'heartily desire' Henry's reign 'to continue for ever', had to make provision for Henry dying without heirs. In such sad circumstances they proposed to avoid a ruinous struggle for the throne by giving Henry full power and authority 'to give, dispose, appoint, assign, declare, and limit . . . the imperial Crown of this realm . . . to such person or persons as shall please your Highness'. If, when he accepted these extraordinary powers, Henry had in mind his son, Henry Fitzroy, he was soon to be disappointed. That summer the young man died of consumption. He was only 17 years old, but his pale cheeks and sickly looks had always contrasted sharply with the florid countenance of his royal father.

In the same session parliament passed two other acts concerning the constitution. The first gave a future monarch at the age of 24 the right to repeal by proclamation any act passed during his minority. By this law Henry hoped to protect his unborn son's prerogative. The second act, prompted by the recent marriage of Thomas Howard, Norfolk's half-brother, to Henry's niece, Lady Margaret Douglas, made it a treasonable offence for any subject to marry a royal lady without the monarch's permission. On this occasion Henry displayed his usual nervous fear whenever he thought anyone was moving too close to the throne. He imprisoned both Thomas and Margaret for their impetuosity, and a few months later Thomas died in the Tower.

Henry and Jane enjoyed the first summer of their married life. They spent long days on the river or in the hunting field, Jane relishing the novelty of her position, and Henry happy and contented with a wife who lived up to her motto, *Bound to Obey and Serve*. The last six or eight months had wrought a transformation in Henry's life. The disturbing claims and jealousies of Catherine and Anne no longer troubled him. Cromwell had solved his financial problems by filling the treasury with monastic wealth, and Francis I and Charles V had turned against each other so fiercely over the possession of Milan that neither dared say a harsh word against England. Even Pope Paul was showing signs of wanting to be friendly. Unfortunately for Henry, these blessings were offset by other troubles. The plague was about again, and his leg seemed to be getting worse. The ulcer had never healed since his fall, and the pain and inflammation had spread to his other leg. Worse still, at the end of the summer disquieting reports of civil unrest began to come from the north.

Edward Hall was of the opinion that 'the inhabitauntes of the North partes' were 'very ignorant and rude, knowing not what true religion meant, but altogether noseled in supersticion and popery'. But Hall was a Londoner, an enthusiast for the 'divinity' of the crown, and a religious reformer. He cannot be expected to share or even understand the fears and apprehension which were disturbing the minds of hundreds of northern gentlemen who distrusted change. They looked askance at the increasing centralisation of government and the corresponding weakening of feudal allegiances. In their eyes the new statute of uses was an attack on the traditional liberties of landowners. They fully understood why such respected, northern leaders as Lords Darcy and Hussey and Sir Thomas Percy grumbled about the advice ministers were giving the king. In some parts of the north men were angry about the new enclosures, in others about recent government regulations concerning weaving, and everywhere about the increasing weight of taxation. They were puzzled and fearful about the new relationship between church and state, and ready to swallow such rumours as that Cromwell and Cranmer were planning to transfer all ecclesiastical wealth to the crown, and close and pull down the parish churches. The arrival of commissioners in 1535 and 1536 supported these alarming reports; the suppression of the lesser houses confirmed them. 'Alacke, alacke!', they cried in their marching song, 'for the church sake, pore comons wake.'

This widespread distemper came to a head first in Lincolnshire and then in Yorkshire. On 1 October rioters at Louth began to march on Lincoln. They proclaimed their intention of saving Henry from the evil control of Cromwell and Cranmer, and they demanded that the suppression of monasteries should cease, and that those responsible for the suppression, especially Drs. Legh and Layton, the two chief visitors in the north, should be punished. Henry's only reply to their pathetic concern for his welfare was abuse, threats, and as rapid a concentration of troops in Lincoln as he could muster. Within three weeks the rioters, who had forced many unwilling gentlemen, abbots, and monks to join them, had dispersed. Their extravagant and violent intentions had evaporated, and each rebel was doing his best to disavow the part he had taken in the rising. But at that very moment, a second revolt, the more serious and deep-rooted Pilgrimage of Grace, was developing further north. It found a responsible leader in Robert Aske, a Yorkshire lawyer. His one aim was to prevent further 'deterioration' in the English church by freeing it from the new secular stranglehold, and by restoring the suppressed monasteries. Aske spoke of his followers not as rebels but as pilgrims, and he chose as his banner a representation of the five wounds of Christ. But such singleness of purpose did not move either Lord Darcy, Aske's chief patron, or many of the 30,000 armed men who came from all parts of the north to support the revolt. They had economic and political scores to settle as well.

Norfolk met Aske at Doncaster on 27 October. He had to play for time because he had too few troops to disperse the rebels. Aske professed loyalty to the crown, and because he believed Henry would seriously consider his demands, he agreed to withdraw and prepare a full statement of them. At the beginning of December, he presented them to Norfolk. They included the repeal of the statute of uses and the dismissal of Cromwell, as well as the restoration of both papal jurisdiction and the suppressed monasteries. Norfolk skilfully turned away the rebels' wrath with vague promises that Henry would visit the northern counties, and that parliament would be asked to reconsider the liberties of the church, so that, protected by a free pardon, Aske ended his pilgrimage and dispersed his well-disciplined followers. Henry summoned him to London, and in apparently friendly fashion listened to his account of the northerners' complaints. But after Aske had returned to Yorkshire and the government showed no signs of fulfilling its promises, some of the more impatient rebels broke the truce. In January 1537 Sir Francis Bigod and John Hallam made an unsuccessful bid to take Scarborough and Hull. There was trouble at Watton Priory and Jervaulx Abbey, and in February hopeless rebellion broke out in Cumberland and Westmorland. Henry seized upon these disturbances as an excuse for ignoring the promises made to Aske, and in the spring and summer of 1537 Norfolk and others held summary courts throughout the northern counties. Aske at York, Darcy at Tower Hill, and a number of abbots and monks both in the north and in London were among the 250 victims executed.

The northern rising had caught the government militarily unprepared, and though the south, apart from the extreme south-west, showed no signs of restlessness, Cromwell, Norfolk, and other ministers must have endured some weeks of trepidation. If Henry shared their alarm and anxiety he gave little sign of doing so. Any fear he might have felt he camouflaged with temper and threats. 'I would rather sell all my plate than these rebels should not be put down', he declared, and from the beginning he was ready to bully the insurgents into submission. 'We marvel what madness is in your brain', he told the 'rude commons' of Lincolnshire 'one of the most brute and beastly [shires] of the whole realm'. On the dissolution of the monasteries he argued:

> And where ye allege that the service of God is much thereby diminished, the truth thereof is contrary ... what unkindness and unnaturality may we impute to you ... that had liefer [rather] such an unthrifty sort of vicious persons should enjoy such possessions ... than we your natural Prince, Sovereign Lord, and King, which doth and hath spent more in your defences, of his own, that six times they be worth.

He never intended to yield an inch. When the Pilgrimage looked most threatening he wrote to Sir William Fitzwilliam, 'ascertain you plainly of our mind in that point touching the Abbeys, we shall never consent to their desires therein ... but adhere to our right therein to the uttermost, being as greatly entitled thereunto as to the Imperial crown of this our realm ...'. And once he had a pretext for breaking the vague promises made in his name, he fully determined to wreak full vengeance. He instructed Norfolk to 'cause such dreadful execution to be done upon a good number of the inhabitants of every town, village, and hamlet that have offended in this rebellion, as well as by hanging them on trees as by the quartering of them, and the setting of their heads and quarters in every town. ...' In particular he was anxious that the religious, whom he wrongly regarded as the instigators of the revolts, should not be spared. When the monks of the small Cistercian monastery of Sawley returned to their suppressed house, Henry sent instructions to the earl of Derby to 'cause the said Abbot and certain of the chief of the monks to be hanged upon long pieces of timber, or otherwise, out of the steeple', and he ordered Norfolk to show no pity on the monks of any house that had resisted his commissioners. Norfolk interpreted his orders pretty generously. His punitive tour of the north so dispirited monks throughout the country that Cromwell's plan to carry out the total dissolution in carefully arranged stages was jostled out of schedule.

A number of large monasteries in the north had held aloof from the Pilgrimage in the selfish belief that since the act of suppression did not apply to them, they would be wise to co-operate with the crown to save their own skins. The community of Furness Abbey, however, held the contrary point of view that the Pilgrimage was the last hope for English monasticism. Therefore when Sussex arrived in that remote part of Lancashire in the spring of 1537, he found Abbot Pyle and his monks, though innocent of any known offence, ready to sign a deed of surrender by which each assigned to the crown 'all such interest and title as I have had, have, or may have in the abbey'. This surrender set a precedent, and throughout the next three years royal commissioners gradually took over every monastery and friary. Not all the heads of houses were as amenable as Abbot Pyle, but only against a dozen monasteries, including Colchester, Glastonbury, and Reading, had the crown to use or threaten to use the force of the law and gallows. By Easter 1540, the last house, the rich, Augustinian, Waltham Abbey, had surrendered, and the transformation of ecclesiastical England had been achieved much more easily and much more quickly than either Cromwell or Henry dared have hoped three or four years earlier. Already it was evident that the crown had been enriched by more than £100,000 a year, even after taking into account gifts made by Henry and the expense of creating six new cathedrals and dioceses. To a king increasingly obsessed with the love of money and struggling with the financial problems of an inflationary world such a gain was a major blessing.

The Birth of Edward VI

Plague had been Henry's first reason for postponing the coronation of his new queen. The northern rising delayed it further, and then Jane's pregnancy, which her delighted husband announced to the world with a service of thanksgiving, cancelled plans for a summer coronation. Henry had promised Aske that Jane should be crowned at York, but

Aske was dead and it seemed foolish to subject Jane to unnecessary strain. Further, he himself did not want to travel north. He found a restricted amount of hunting and riding painful enough, and since his appetite seemed to grow as his exercise diminished, he was fast putting on weight. He spent his summer relatively quietly never far away from his queen, hoping, dreaming, and praying for the safe delivery of the child she was carrying. On 12 October 1537 at Hampton Court, after a protracted labour Jane gave birth to a son. Singing, bell-ringing, gun-firing, cheering, and feasting all marked the joyous occasion. Three days later the baby was christened *Edward*, both because he had been born on the eve of St. Edward's day, and because Henry wished to honour the memory of his grandfather, Edward IV. Norfolk, Suffolk, and Cranmer stood as godfathers, and Mary and Elizabeth were among the distinguished guests. But Jane was not there. She was lying on her bed in the grip of puerperal fever, and on 25 October she died. For the first time in his life Henry knew the grief of losing a loved one. He ordered that Jane's body should lie three weeks in state before it was taken to Windsor for burial, and he received the congratulations which Francis sent him on the birth of Edward with the words, '. . . Divine Providence hath mingled my joy with the bitterness of the death of her who brought me this happiness'. For once a diplomatic dispatch might be accepted at its face value.

Threat of Invasion

Because they were at war with each other in Picardy and Piedmont, neither Francis I nor Charles V had been able to take advantage of Henry's vulnerability during the days of the northern rising, and for fear of driving Henry into an alliance with the other, neither had even dared give any encouragement to Reginald Pole, the grandson of Edward IV's brother, Clarence. Paul III had created Pole a cardinal, and had sent him far too late to the Netherlands in the vain hope of finding ways of helping the insurgents in the northern counties. It would have suited Henry if Francis and Charles could have remained at each other's throats for the rest of their lives, but inevitably their enthusiasm for expensive war began to flag. By the autumn of 1537, despite all Henry's diplomatic efforts to keep the fighting going, the end of the campaigning was clearly in sight. Henry decided it would be wise to change his tactics and offer his services as a peace-maker. Through Sir Thomas Wyatt, his ambassador in Spain, he told Charles that he would be 'right glad to take upon us the office of a mediator', but he queered his pitch somewhat when he boastingly added that Charles 'could not in Christendom have chosen an arbiter of such honour as we be, ne one to whom he hath more cause to show all gratuity and kindness that he could imagine, than to us'. At all costs Henry wished to avoid isolation, especially if the pope had any chance of forming a triple alliance against him. He had three children to offer in marriage, but he thought his best policy was to exploit his own new status as a widower.

To Henry's surprise, neither Charles nor Francis seemed to value a marriage alliance with England's king too highly. With every confidence that he was bestowing a great favour on France, Henry requested the hand of Mary of Guise. He picked on this comparatively distant relative of Francis I because she had recently become engaged to James V, and he was anxious to stifle the dangerous, growing friendship between France and Scotland. But instead of suspending negotiations with James and eagerly discussing Henry's flattering offer, Francis startled Henry by continuing to steer Franco-Scottish negotiations into a firm alliance. Francis also dismissed Henry's outrageous suggestion that he should send a selection of eligible French ladies to Calais for inspection: 'trotting out the young ladies like geldings'—as Francis inelegantly put it—would have made little appeal to him however eager he had been for a union with England.

Hopes of a marriage alliance with the Empire were equally slender. Wyatt, following Henry's instructions, suggested as if 'out of his own head' that Christina, the tall, young widow of Francesco Sforza, would make Henry a suitable wife. Charles professed he was ready to give his consent. Indeed between January and April 1538, this and other Imperial alliances with Mary, Elizabeth, and Edward were repeatedly discussed, but Charles had little interest in them. He probably regarded them chiefly as a means of pressing Francis into line, and when it began to look as if these proposed marriages would not create a strong Anglo-Imperial front against France, Henry too dismissed them from his mind. Events forced him to realise that he was impotent to prevent Francis and Charles from making peace. In June 1538 Paul III negotiated a formal truce between them at Nice. Later that month emperor and king spent three days together at Aigues-Mortes in Languedoc vowing to be firm friends, and expressing mutual shock and horror at news from England about the dissolution of monasteries and the desecration of shrines. Before they parted they agreed to ask the pope to publish the suspended bull of excommunication against Henry. It is likely that Henry received reports of this meeting with a chuckle, because no one knew better than he how much pretence there was bound to be at Aigues-Mortes. He did not forget that the Turks were still pressing up the Danube valley, that the Netherlanders opposed the idea of war with England, and that the fundamental, conflicting interests of France and the Empire in so many areas of Europe could not help but be flaws in any alliance. But he took things more seriously when he received reports that Paul III was trying to persuade James V to invade England from the north, that Pole had undertaken another papal mission to stir up England's enemies, and that at Toledo in January 1539 Francis and Charles had expressly agreed not to come to any understanding with Henry without the other's consent.

Once he realised that a joint attack against England was possible if not probable, Henry began to take precautionary measures. Partly through commissioners and partly by personal inspection which necessitated 'very laborious and paineful journeies towardes the sea coastes' during the summer of 1538, he ordered and encouraged squads of local workmen to repair defences along the whole length of the south and east coasts, across the Channel round Calais, and on the Scottish border. The county militias mustered for inspection, and Henry personally saw to it that his port officers held ships and men in readiness to sail at short notice under the command of the high admiral, the earl of Southampton. All this activity roused widespread patriotic enthusiasm, for no one wished to suffer invasion. Excitement increased when it became known that Continental clergy were paying special war taxes, and that the emperor was accumulating guns and ammunition in the Antwerp area. Merchants and seafarers were particularly enraged when the emperor later, in the early months of 1539, seized all English ships in Flemish and Spanish ports. It is hardly surprising that, apart from a few aristocratic tongues cursing the upstart Cromwell, no one in this tense atmosphere objected when Henry and Cromwell took swift and terrible action against Cardinal Pole's English relations. They arrested his brother Geoffrey, and on the evidence they squeezed and battered out of him, they shut his mother, the elderly countess of Salisbury, in the Tower, and on 9 December 1538 executed his eldest brother, Lord Montague, and the marquis of Exeter. Most men seemed to regard this as a necessary if unhappy precaution, the stifling of a fifth column before it could do any mischief.

Abroad Henry handled his diplomatic correspondence with supreme confidence. Cromwell, far more apprehensive than Henry, feared to think what England would suffer if pope, king, and emperor formed an active Catholic triumvirate against her. But Henry chose to view foreign affairs as a personal matter between crowned heads. Practical factors of distance and time unfortunately compelled sovereigns to employ ministers and ambassadors in diplomatic work, but he kept in mind that none of his servants had enjoyed half his own long experience in negotiating with his brother monarchs. During the winter months of 1538–9 he spent many busy hours writing personal letters to Charles and revising dispatches to his ambassadors. He still harped upon his proposed marriage with Christina, but behind the pretences, circumlocutions, and diplomatic protests, his chief purpose seems to have been to gain time. With his tongue in his cheek, he complained loudly about delays—'. . . we cannot a little marvel of the very frosty coldness and slack remissness they show now, in very deed far from the correspondence of the sincerity we looked to have had . . . .' He accused Charles of 'knitting one delay to the tail of another', and he instructed Thomas Wriothesley and Stephen Vaughan, two of his envoys in the Netherlands, to assure Christina 'how earnestly we have been minded to honour her by our marriage'. He pointed out that if they skilfully showed whose fault it was that the marriage now [Christmas 1539] appeared so doubtful, they might 'not only print in her heart our loving and gentle proceedings . . . but also conceive a grudge . . . to them that have been letters [hinderers] of such honourable and commodious alliances'. He countered the influence of Pole by announcing abroad that an English court had found him guilty of treason, and by warning Charles that the cardinal would take every opportunity 'to weep crocodile tears' and to 'pour forth the venom of his serpent nature'. Henry was prepared to be patient, but he could act promptly and firmly when he considered it necessary to do so. He quickly arrested Flemish and Spanish ships as a reprisal, and he utterly refused to agree that his proposed marriage with Christina required a dispensation from 'the bishop of Rome'. Amply reinforced by the Turkish threat, by the commercial interests of the Netherlanders, and by Charles's mistrust of France and the Lutheran princes, Henry's mixture of confidence and precaution achieved success. By Easter 1539 it was clear that Charles had called off the invasion at least for the present. The Imperial war fleet had been dispersed, the impounded English ships set free, and the pope still thought it unwise to issue the bull against Henry.

The *Henry Grâce-à-Dieu*, 1512

6 ACTIVITY IN SPITE OF INFIRMITY

'. . . every part about you blasted with antiquity.'
SHAKESPEARE

HAD Cromwell had his way, from the first Henry would have been seeking to force the emperor's hand by allying with the German princes. Henry was reluctant to do this because of his hatred of Lutheranism, but in January 1539, during the darkest days of the invasion scare when both Francis and Charles recalled their ambassadors from London, he allowed himself to be persuaded that he should form a precautionary alliance with Denmark and the Protestant German princes. Cromwell argued that Henry might cement this alliance by marrying Anne, the sister of the duke of Cleves. The duke was a mild reformer, and his lands to the north-east of the Netherlands were strategically placed for an invasion of the emperor's dominions if the need arose. From a political point of view Henry agreed that there were temporary advantages, but he never shared Cromwell's apparent indifference to the religious difficulties inherent in the proposed alliance.

In theological matters Henry considered himself an even greater authority and master than in foreign diplomacy. Age had sharpened rather than dulled his interest in the subject, but his toleration of opposition was less than ever. He took his title, *Supreme Head of the Church of England*, quite literally, and considered it axiomatic that he should decide what his subjects believed and how they worshipped. Like most of his contemporaries, Henry rejected the very concept of personal liberty in theological matters, and in 1536 he put before convocation the Ten Articles. This statement of belief upheld the essentials of traditional doctrine on the three sacraments of the altar, penance, and baptism, but it also initiated certain practical reforms. Images were to be retained, but superstitious reverence of them forbidden: prayers were still to be offered for the souls of the dead, but no one was to believe that masses could facilitate a soul's passage through purgatory. In 1537 the traditionalists scored a point when Henry permitted the publication of *The Institution of a Christian Man*, an orthodox statement on belief and liturgy, but the reformers drew even again when he granted their request for an English Bible. Once some publication difficulties had been overcome, the Great Bible, a part-Tyndale part-Coverdale translation, was chained to the lectern in English churches, and parish priests began to teach their parishioners the Lord's Prayer, the Creed, and the Commandments in the vulgar tongue. During the summer of 1538 deputies from the German states—forerunners, Cromwell hoped, of treaty makers—came to England to discuss theological problems with Cranmer and other bishops. They achieved no profitable conclusions partly because the Englishmen dared not commit themselves before Henry had spoken. Henry remained silent because he did not wish to aggravate his diplomatic difficulties in Europe, but in November, after the Germans had returned home, he banned the importation and printing of books 'contrary to the true faith, reverence and due observation of such sacraments and sacramentals and laudable rites, ceremonies, as heretofore have been used and accustomed with the Church of England'. He confessed that he abhorred Anabaptists and Sacramentaries and 'their wicked and abominable errors and opinions', and he upheld the doctrine of transubstantiation, the celibacy of the clergy, and the traditional liturgy of the church. Yet at the same time, with the king's hearty approval, Cromwell and Cranmer were supervising the dissolution of the greater monasteries, and conducting an iconoclastic campaign against images and shrines.

Henry summoned parliament to meet in April 1539, when the threat of invasion had diminished, but when a second theological mission had arrived from Germany and his ministers were taking the first steps towards an alliance with the Lutheran princes. He asked lords and commons to consider 'the diversities of opinions' that had lately sprung up in England upon religious matters, but, as he deemed it his right and duty to do, he left members in no doubt of his own views. He believed that too free a reading of the Bible caused heterodox ideas. God's word did not compel him 'to set forth the Scripture in English to his lay subjects'. He had done it 'of his own liberality and goodness', and his subjects should 'use the holy Scripture in English according to his godly purpose and gracious intent'. Even to the extreme of speaking in the house of lords, Henry guided parliament into passing the act of six articles, which, under mounting penalties of fine, imprisonment, and death, insisted that Englishmen should accept traditionalist doctrine on transubstantiation, clerical celibacy, confession, and private masses. Cranmer and Latimer did not approve of this 'whip with six strings', but later in convocation they found that they had little support among the bishops, and in the parishes hardly any sympathy from either priests or influential laity. Cromwell preferred reformist to traditional doctrine, but his chief worry was that this new reactionary law might ruin the foreign policy he was advocating.

Anne of Cleves

The marriage treaty between Henry and Anne of Cleves was signed on 6 October 1539. Anne broke the promises made on her behalf that she would marry the duke of Lorraine's son, and Henry agreed not to ask for a dowry. He seemed unduly excited at the prospect of meeting his new wife. It had been arranged that he should welcome her with appropriate ceremony when she reached Blackheath, but he could not resist anticipating their meeting by paying her a private, surprise visit at Rochester. Her appearance and the prospect of marrying her left him 'marvellously astonished and abashed'. Holbein, whom Henry considered 'very excellent in making Physiognomies', had painted her portrait, and Dr. Nicholas Wotton, an ambassador, had sent him a written description. Neither had been very flattering. Henry also had known that she was 34 years old. But quite clearly he had never expected so ugly, ungainly, and ill-dressed a bride. The ladies who accompanied her made matters no better. Like Anne herself they understood no English, and no one understood their German. Their foreign fashions, heavy features, and incomprehensible chatter were bound to provoke ridicule and banter in London and at court. Henry confessed to Cromwell that if he had known what Anne was like, he would never have consented to the match, but he allowed none of this resentment and disappointment to appear in public. At Blackheath he greeted his bride with every courtesy, and 'with moste lovely countenaunce and Princely behaviour saluted, welcomed and embrased her to the great rejoysyng of the beholders', and though the wedding was postponed a little in the desperate hope that some way might be found of cancelling it without insulting the duke of Cleves and his allies beyond repair, he married her at Greenwich on 6 January 1540 with all fitting ceremony and splendour. Hall, who never missed an opportunity of describing festival occasions in great detail, said that Anne was 'apparelled in a gowne of ryche cloth of gold set full of large flowers of great and Orient Pearle, made after the Duche fassion rownde, her here hangyng doune, whiche was faire, yellow and long'. Henry outshone her with his crimson satin coat, his gown of cloth of gold, and the 'ryche coller about his necke'. Outwardly all seemed well, but Henry did not attempt to hide his feelings from his councillors. Norfolk, Gardiner, and others who, like them, detested both Cromwell and his policy, thought that in Henry's disappointment there was hope of recovering their lost authority. Long-standing differences on theology were now buttressed by divisions on foreign policy, and during the next six months both factions battled for power. Henry must have been fully aware of what was happening, but he stood aside and contentedly accepted profits and presents from both sides.

In February 1540 Norfolk brought back from the French court a strong impression that, though Francis disapproved of Cromwell's ecclesiastical policy, there was little likelihood of him joining an alliance against England. Henry accepted this opinion as his own, for he could see signs of the old rivalry between Francis and Charles reappearing, and he felt confident that he could help it grow. The need for an alliance with Cleves had passed, if ever it had existed. In the near future it was likely to be a diplomatic burden, just as Anne was a matrimonial burden. He had recently met Catherine Howard, a young, sprightly niece of the duke of Norfolk. Gardiner and all the Howards hoped great things of Catherine's ability to fascinate the king. Probably Gardiner's restoration to the privy council was a first fruit, and his theological-political victory over Dr. Barnes, Cromwell's protégé, a second. But Cromwell still exerted great power. He was playing down the act of the six articles very successfully, and he had prosecuted several prominent men for going too far in supporting the Catholic reaction. In April he persuaded the commons to vote substantial taxes, and he received the earldom of Essex for pouring the treasures of the dissolved order of the Knights of St. John into the royal exchequer. In May he convinced Henry that he should imprison in the Tower

King Henry the eyght.

HENRY VIII IN COUNCIL
Woodcut by Jacob Faber in Edward Hall's 'Chronicle', 1548

Richard Sampson, the newly created bishop of Chichester and a friend of Gardiner. If Cromwell could only have found a way of ridding Henry of this Queen Anne as he had done the other, he would have weathered these bad days, but so long as Anne remained queen his enemies had too many advantages. Early in June they triumphed.

Suddenly and unexpectedly Cromwell found himself arrested at a meeting of the council. His wealth was declared confiscate to the crown, and he was imprisoned in the Tower charged with treason for 'counter working the King's aims for the settlement of religion', and for having said that he would resist 'if the King and the realm varied from his opinions'. The court condemned him to death without hearing a word in his defence. As he waited for the day of execution, Cromwell searched his memory and wracked his brain for evidence to help Henry dissolve his marriage. This last service did not save him, and the axe ended his life at Tyburn on 28 July 1540. As many of his contemporaries did, and in a style reminiscent of Stalin's victims, he spent his last few minutes of life confessing his offences, and asking the onlookers to pray for his forgiveness and 'for the Kynges grace, that he maie long live with you, in healthe and prosperitie'. He died mourned by very few. Among the nobles and clergy he had made many enemies. Cranmer, his ally in much of his work, made no attempt to defend him, and Henry, who owed his new wealth and some of his un-questioned supremacy to his skill, showed him no pity and quickly dismissed him from his mind.

With his usual lack of feeling for what was appropriate, Henry chose Cromwell's execution day as his wedding day to Catherine Howard. After Cromwell's arrest, Gardiner had guided and pushed convocation into declaring Henry's marriage to Anne null and void. It appeared that the king had only married her on condition that she obtained release from her former engagement to the son of the duke of Lorraine. Moreover, hostile threats from Charles and Francis had forced him to marry her, so that he had lacked 'inward consent', and accordingly had never consummated the marriage. 'I never for love to the Woman consented to marry', Henry told his subjects in a public declaration, 'nor yet if she brought maidenhead with her, took any from her by true carnal copulation.' Anne raised no objections to these statements. She quickly settled down to enjoy her two manors of Richmond and Blechingly and her £4,000 a year, and apparently preferred to be Henry's 'right dear and right entirely beloved sister', as he addressed her, than the queen of so dangerous and unpredictable a king. A few weeks later, Marillac, the French ambassador, reported, 'As to her who is now called Madame de Cleves, far from pretending to be married, she is as joyous as ever, and wears new dresses every day.' Her happy acceptance of the inevitable, so different from Queen Catherine's stubborn hostility, filled Henry's heart with pleasure and admiration for her. The only angry person in the whole affair was the duke of Cleves, and his anger no longer disturbed Henry. Negotiations between England and the Empire had already become friendly enough for Charles to declare himself Henry's 'loving brother and most cordial friend'.

A Second Queen Catherine

Catherine Howard for Anne of Cleves seemed to Henry a most satisfactory exchange. This fifth wife, still in her early twenties, was gay, attractive, vivacious, and very good company. He could not keep his hands from fondling her, and his eyes from finding gifts to please her. She brought with her no awkward obligations to foreign princes, and her love of traditional forms of worship ensured that she would not encourage dangerous reformers. She was as great a comfort and joy as Jane had been. She had grown up in the household of her grandmother, the dowager duchess of Norfolk and widow of the victor of Flodden. Her uncle, Norfolk, thought well of her, and Gardiner apparently approved of her as queen. Henry would often be seeking the advice of both duke and bishop, but he had no intention of allowing either of them to inherit Cromwell's authority. He alone would henceforward direct foreign policy, and now that the new church had set its course and trimmed its sails, he had no need to fill the office of vicegerent left vacant by Cromwell's dismissal. Henry's new happiness showed itself in his improved health. In the late summer the plague returned to London, and as usual Henry retreated before it. But this time he found compensating pleasure in hawking and riding, and in the new gaiety of the court. Despite his game leg and his growing paunch, he set himself an exacting daily routine. According to Marillac, he wakened between 5 and 6 o'clock, heard mass at 7, and then rode until dinner-time at 10 o'clock. After dinner he was ready to deal with the business of the day.

26, 27 HENRY WITH HIS
JESTER, AND (BELOW)
READING
*Both from a psalter made
for Henry's own use by
John Mallard*

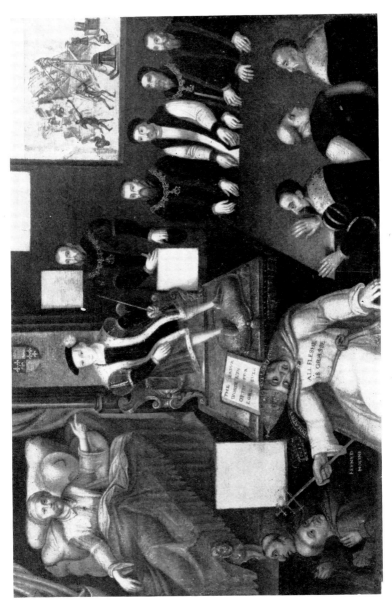

28 'THE PROTESTANT SUCCESSION'. HENRY ON HIS DEATHBED, WITH EDWARD VI AND THE COUNCIL

From an anonymous painting

Much of the business concerned foreign affairs. Henry rejected all thought of further association with the Protestant princes. He pressed for an alliance with the emperor, and therefore had to look out sharply for plans Francis might be hatching with James of Scotland. Ireland too was a troublesome running sore. The chieftains were in revolt again. Henry believed this was due to the treachery of his deputy, Lord Leonard Grey. Therefore he sent Grey to the Tower, and appointed Sir Anthony St. Leger in his stead. By bribing the malcontents with titles and with lands taken from suppressed monasteries, St. Leger achieved some temporary success, and he pleased Henry again when he advised him to assume two new titles—*King of Ireland* instead of his old *Lord of Ireland*, and *Head of the Irish Church*. Domestic affairs also brought their problems. Although he never altered his intention of enforcing uniformity of belief and practice in his church, Henry could not ignore the marked differences of opinion and outlook among his bishops and councillors. For the moment the best he could do, he decided, was to cut down any extreme or extravagant growth as soon as it appeared. Almost symbolically, two days after Cromwell's execution, he had six people put to death at Smithfield with a nice, if horrifying impartiality: three were hanged for speaking in favour of the pope, and three, including Barnes, Gardiner's old opponent, were burned alive for holding heretical, Protestant opinions. The degree of difference between the policies advocated by Cranmer and Gardiner he could just about tolerate, and he found advantages and some satisfaction in holding a balance between them.

In March 1541 Henry fell ill. His winter exercise had not reduced his girth—from his armour it has been calculated that he had added 17 inches to his waist measurement since 1536—and suddenly his ulcerated legs became acutely painful. A high temperature confined him to bed, and made him depressed, full of self-pity, and more than usually irritable. According to the French ambassador he was 'often of a different opinion in the morning than after dinner'. News that another revolt had broken out in the north increased his dangerous anger. No one felt safe during those spring months, for Henry reckoned other people's life and liberty of little account. A rumoured word of disloyalty was enough to commit a man to the Tower and possibly to the block. Those whom Cromwell had trusted were particularly vulnerable to rumour. Though they were later released, Wallop, Wyatt, and the king's two secretaries, Wriothesley and Sadler, all spent anxious days in the Tower. Leonard Grey, Lord Dacres, and the 70-year-old countess of Salisbury were not so fortunate: they were executed.

As the days lengthened Henry recovered his health again, and in high summer he and Catherine, accompanied by an entourage of 4000 or 5000, left London for their promised but long-postponed visit to the northern counties. Everywhere Henry went men made their submission and offered gifts to atone for the north's recent misdeeds: each town presented its quota of kneeling penitents and, just as important, its bag of gold. Stamford, Lincoln, and Boston gave £20, £40, and £50 respectively. Lindsey subscribed £300, and the archbishop of York, on behalf of the northern province, tendered twice that sum. York, Newcastle, and Hull enriched the treasury with £100 each. It was a most satisfactory progress in every sense. Henry was feeling better in himself, and was very happy with Catherine. The only disappointment of the whole tour was that James V failed to keep his promise to meet his uncle at York. Henry had always considered his nephew most wilful, but this time he rightly suspected that his broken promise was not unconnected with French instructions.

Henry arrived back at Hampton Court at the end of October 1541. Bad news greeted him for his son, Edward, was not well, and his sister, Queen Margaret of Scotland, had died. But a few days later these seemed trifling worries. In church on All Souls' Day, Cranmer nervously placed in his hand a written statement accusing his well-beloved Catherine of infidelity. Henry could not believe it, but Cranmer, who spoke for Audley and Edward Seymour as well, produced his evidence and his witnesses. Henry ordered the arrest and strict examination of the key persons—Mary Lassells, the ex-nurse in the household of the duchess of Norfolk, Henry Manox, Catherine's young music master, and Francis Dereham, a poor relation of the Howards. Catherine herself was confined to her rooms, but a few days later Norfolk and Cranmer questioned her closely. She confessed that before her marriage she had been Dereham's mistress. Dereham had already admitted this, and Manox boasted that at one time he too had been very familiar with her. Worse followed, for further searching inquiries revealed that since she became queen, Catherine had secretly been meeting Thomas Culpeper, a young and handsome gentleman of the chamber. At Catherine's urgent request, Lady Rochford had contrived to arrange these clandestine meetings even on the recent royal progress in the north. This culminating evidence broke Henry altogether. He wept in his seat at the council table, and afterwards alternated between bouts of anger, in one of which he threatened to have Catherine tortured to death, and spells of self-pity when he complained about the ill-luck he had had in his choice of wives, and grumbled that his council constantly advised him badly. Chapuys was among those who recorded how Henry showed greater sorrow at Catherine's loss 'than at the faults, loss, or divorce of his preceding wives', though cynically he attributed this sorrow to the fact that 'as yet this king has formed neither a plan nor a preference' for marrying again.

There could only be one gloomy end to the Catherine affair, but there was no reason, as in Anne Boleyn's case, to rush through the judicial proceedings. Dereham and Culpeper were tried at Guildhall on 1 December 1541. They both pleaded guilty, though Culpeper denied that Catherine had committed adultery with him. Before her marriage he had wished to make her his wife. He still loved her, but since her marriage to Henry, they had done nothing worse than exchange letters and meet occasionally in private. Both men were executed at Tyburn ten days later. Meanwhile, Catherine was being held a prisoner at Syon, the now deserted Brigettine convent, and Henry left London for the country. He spent a melancholy Christmas. In January 1542, as he had planned, parliament took the final matters out of his hands. After members of the privy council had questioned Catherine further, lords and commons passed a bill of attainder against her. For the first time ever, Henry gave his assent to a bill not in person but through a commission of peers. Catherine was transferred from Syon to the Tower, and on 13 February she and Lady Rochford were executed, like Anne Boleyn, on Tower Green. 'I loved Culpeper', Catherine confessed, 'and I wish to God I had done as he wished me, for at the time the king wanted to take me, he urged me to say I was pledged to him.'

War Against Scotland

The one piece of good news which partially consoled Henry at Christmastide 1541 was that Francis and Charles were once again bitterly opposed to each other. Two envoys, whom Francis had sent to negotiate a renewal of his alliance with the Turks, had been seized and executed by the Spanish governor of Milan. This aggressive act had shattered the tenuous peace which had existed since the Treaty of Nice, and once again Henry could begin trying to sell his support to the monarch who had most to offer. This time he turned first to Charles. Francis was known to be seeking the alliance of Cleves, and Cleves was too sharp and disastrous a memory for Henry to put out of his mind. Worse still, for some time and with some success, Francis had been trying to persuade the Scots to invade England.

In 1540 Henry had sent Ralph Sadler to Scotland both to advise his nephew, James V, that he could do no better in church matters than follow his uncle's excellent example, and to warn him against the fickleness of Continental allies. 'To speak of the Emperor, or the French King, what can he look for at either, or at both their hands, but fair words and entertainment for a time, as their instruments with his own danger to serve their purposes.' Henry had bidden Sadler point out the three-fold advantages of an English alliance—peace, ready help when necessary, and avuncular affection. But neither Sadler's mission nor Henry's later letters had won Scotland's co-operation. James V seemed dominated by the pro-French cardinal, David Beaton, archbishop of St. Andrews, and in no way attracted by any of Henry's proposals. As he had demonstrated on other occasions, Henry could show remarkable official patience, but the Scots had worn it dangerously thin by the spring of 1542. James's admission that before he could meet Henry he must consult Francis provoked Henry's withering reply that he would 'be loath to put him to so great pains . . . we thought verily that he neither needed nor would have asked advice of any other prince to have met with such an uncle as since his tender age hath showed himself so careful over him as few in Christendom hath showed the like'. After this, Anglo-Scottish relations deteriorated rapidly, and in the late summer Henry declared war. In a long, detailed vindication he 'thought good to notify unto the world' why he had taken this step, which hitherto he had 'so much abhorred and fled'. James IV, the present king's father, had been churlish enough to invade England after he had been accorded the signal honour of marrying Margaret Tudor, and his death at Flodden had been a 'due punishment of God'. With unparalleled generosity Henry had not allowed this crime to prevent him from 'nourishing' the sinner's son, for he had hoped that that tree which 'was of the one part of so good a stock' would eventually bring forth good fruit. But his hopes had been blasted. While professing friendship for his uncle, James V had sheltered English rebels, plotted against English interests, and raided across the border. Henry had 'patiently suffered many delusions', but now reluctantly and lamentably he had decided that he had no alternative but to use 'our force and puissance against him, not for revengence of our private displeasure, but for recovery of our right'. Henry knew that God would help him to advance right against 'wrong, falsehood, deceit, and dissimulation'.

Thomas Cromwell had helped Henry to see a vision of a British Isles united in a single administration under an English king. In the 'thirties both men had advanced towards this ideal by destroying local franchises in England, especially that of the palatinate of Durham, and by enforcing English law and local government throughout Wales. Early in the 'forties St. Leger had integrated Ireland more closely into English government, and in this declaration of war against Scotland late in 1542, Henry revived the old claim of the English monarch to be suzerain of Scotland. He reminded everyone that 'the passing over of time . . . is not allegeable in prescription for the loss of any right', and he claimed that he was entitled to full compensation for not receiving from the Scots the revenue due to the suzerain during the long minority of James V.

The fighting was quickly over. In October 1542 Norfolk advanced across the border, and after burning villages and ravaging the country-side withdrew to Berwick. The next month James attacked on the extreme west, but Sir Thomas Wharton, the warden of the western marches, aided by a rapidly advancing tide, trapped the Scottish army in the mud of the Solway estuary. Hundreds of Scottish nobles and gentlemen surrendered. James V, only 30 years of age, died of fever aggravated by despair, and left to succeed him his only child, the four-days-old Mary. Henry professed feeling a sense of family loss in the death of his nephew, but politically he could have asked for nothing better. Edward could now marry the infant Mary, and their heir could inherit both kingdoms. This would entail the separation of Scotland from the Roman church, and, thought Henry, the education of Mary in England. The earls of Cassilis and Glencairn and other notable prisoners captured at Solway Moss recovered their freedom by under-taking to work for this political plan in Scotland. Should the infant queen not survive, they were told, then Henry would 'take the whole

rule, dominion, and government of that realm upon him that the same
may be governed in peace, tranquillity, and justice'. Henry's 'clemency'
soon showed results. Cardinal Beaton was gaoled, the earl of Arran
was appointed regent, the new Scottish government agreed to accept
the English Bible, and on 1 July the Scots signed the Treaty of Greenwich, which accepted the proposal that eventually Edward and Mary
should marry. Henry yielded one point. He agreed that Mary should be
brought up in Scotland until she was ten years old, but he insisted that
six Scottish noblemen should live at the English court as an earnest
that the Scots intended carrying out the treaty.

Midsummer 1543 found Henry happy and confident. His success
with the Scots pleased him enormously. He flattered himself that he
was handling matters well on the Continent, and he had discovered the
lady whom he intended to make his sixth wife. Since Catherine
Howard's death he had not shunned female company, but he had shown
little desire to choose another wife. He could not prevent the eligible
ladies of the court from indulging in speculation, hope, and dread, but
he probably surprised them all when he decided to marry Catherine
Parr, a thirty-year-old widow, small in stature, and in no way remarkable for her good looks. Catherine had been married twice before,
first to Lord Edward Borough and secondly to Lord Latimer. After
Latimer's death early in 1543 she attracted the eye of Sir Thomas
Seymour, the ambitious, vigorous, younger brother of Jane Seymour,
and destined shortly to become lord admiral. But when Henry asked
her to marry him, she, touched with pity by his obvious need of
affection, put aside her genuine feeling for Seymour, and devoted the
next few years to caring for the needs of the sick king and his three
children. Much later, after Henry's death, she explained to Seymour
that 'God withstood my will therein most vehemently for a time . . .
and made me renounce utterly mine own will, and follow Him most
willingly'. Politics did not interest her. She was an enthusiast for the
new learning, and in theological matters would have liked to see more
reform. But she had no hostility in her. She spoke on church topics
without guile or conscious care, innocently breaking the law on
occasions merely by saying what first came into her mind. Humanity
concerned her far more than theology. Henry married her on 12 July
1543 at Hampton Court. This time Gardiner officiated in place of
Cranmer. The two princesses were present at the quiet, private

ceremony, and nothing marred the gentle happiness of the occasion. The only person who disapproved in the slightest appears to have been Anne of Cleves. 'A fine burthen Madam Catherine hath taken on herself', was her experienced comment.

War Against France

Within a fortnight of marrying Catherine, Henry declared war on France. Negotiations with Charles had been leading up to this for some months, but Henry's timing of the declaration was partly due to excessive confidence which success against the Scots had engendered in him. Ever since the execution of the two French envoys in Milan, the fortunes of the emperor had been sinking steadily. The Turks had advanced further along the Danube valley, the Sultan had defeated Imperial troops in Algiers, and Francis had gained as allies not only the expected Turks and Lutherans but also Venice and the Papacy. Charles had turned to Henry in some despair. Henry was anxious enough to become the full-blooded partner of the emperor, but he had not wished to display his eagerness by rushing into an alliance. Throughout 1542 he had played the diplomat, grasping all possible gains from his temporary advantages, and playing one side off against the other. He had shown no favour either to Chapuys or Marillac. He had corresponded with Francis, and had taken the line that he deplored that 'the state of Christendom should be in such perturbation, and such an entry made to the common enemy of the same, the Turk'. He had not been able to resist reminding Francis that he had previously offered his services as mediator, but '. . . you seemed rather to put your confidence in the Bishop of Rome, so as the sequel declareth the matter to be nothing amended, but in worse terms than it was before'. He had also pressed for the payment of the life-pension Francis had agreed to give him in 1525. At the same time he had proposed to Emperor Charles that they should each declare themselves hostile to the other's enemies, but since this would have required that he should denounce the pope, Charles had shown no willingness to agree. Events had moved further in Henry's favour after Francis had invaded the Netherlands in the summer of 1542, and in February 1543 Charles's desperation had forced him to sign a treaty with England. Henry had not insisted upon Charles denouncing the pope, but the emperor had pledged himself to help

Henry recover his French pension and 'his ancient rights' in France, and had undertaken not to make peace with France without Henry's agreement. From this moment Anglo-French relations steadily deteriorated. Henry seized some French 'pirate ships' off the Isle of Wight, and Francis retaliated by impounding English ships in French ports. In this over-confident mood Henry rejected a belated attempt by Francis to bribe him away from his treaty with Charles, and once fighting began, prestige, honour, and sheer inability to stop it ensured that it would continue. Before long many English people were cursing the day when Henry had involved them in war on the Continent. No great victories and easy ransoms were in sight, and the cost of fighting was too high to be contemplated calmly.

Henry's own elation was short-lived. By August the Scottish situation had gone sour. Regent Arran had misjudged the Scots' willingness to yield to Henry's one-sided terms, and with the support of the church, half the nobility, and French warships in Scottish waters, Cardinal Beaton had forced him to follow a pro-French policy. Scottish government quietly passed from the regent to a council dominated by the cardinal and the queen-mother. Before Christmas the council disowned the Treaty of Greenwich, and renewed Scotland's alliance with France. Henry was threatened with the likelihood of war on two fronts.

For the first 12 months, Henry conducted the war from the English court. In July 1543 he sent Sir John Wallop at the head of 6000 troops to reinforce the Imperial army in the Netherlands, but he himself was busy raising money and trying by promises and threats to prevent the Scottish situation from slipping from bad to worse. The previous year he had levied a forced loan, and, by mixing more alloy with the silver and gold, had begun a ruinous debasement of coinage. The loan raised over £100,000, but neither this nor increased debasement gave Henry anything like enough to meet mounting war expenses. Both parliament and convocation voted supplies, and in 1544 a profitable benevolence brought in more money. Yet frantic insatiable need drove Henry to sell more and more crown lands and to raise loans in the Netherlands at ruinous rates of interest. At length, in 1545, he abolished the chantries despite his belief in purgatory, and the consequent new revenues passed through the treasury into the hands of his creditors. In Henry's last years war devoured the fortune which Cromwell had made for him, just as in earlier years military adventure and gay living had squandered the money which Henry VII had carefully and painfully accumulated.

While he still had hopes that the anti-French party, particularly Angus, Cassilis, Glencairn, and, later, Lennox, might recover the initiative, Henry held his hand against Scotland. But early in 1544 he had to admit that hopes of success were pretty forlorn. Accordingly, he declared war, and in May sent Edward Seymour, earl of Hertford, with a fleet to attack Edinburgh, sack Holyrood House, Leith, and 'as many towns and villages about Edinburgh as you may conveniently'. In particular Hertford was 'so to spoil and turn upset down the Cardinal's town of St. Andrews, as the upper stone may be the nether, and not one stick stands by another, sparing no creature alive within the same, specially such as either in friendship or blood be allied to the Cardinal'. Hertford carried out his orders as completely as he could, but the wanton destruction his troops achieved did not frighten the Scots into submission. Instead it turned many away from their English sympathies. Henry honoured the earl of Lennox with the hand of his niece, Margaret Douglas, and he used money freely to win support for Beaton's opponents, but much of his effort was fruitless. The end of 1544 saw his cause in Scotland no further advanced than it had been at the beginning.

In June 1544, completely against medical advice, the bidding of Charles V, and the wishes of his councillors, Henry insisted upon crossing the Channel to lead his army in battle. He would have gone earlier in the year, if in March his ulcer had not become very painful and forced him to stay in bed. Even on campaign it sometimes compelled him to ride in a litter, and leave the tactical direction of his troops to his two elderly warriors, Norfolk and Suffolk. Through his pain and discomfort Henry seems to have been spurred on by a grotesque illusion that he was following a noble tradition of English monarchs. The war had become quite unnecessary. Francis no longer had heart or body for it. He was offering to discuss peace, and by negotiation Henry could have persuaded him to withdraw French support from Scotland. That would have been a real victory, but instead Henry chose the expensive panoply of war. While the skinny, morose, gouty emperor was striking west through Champagne intending near Paris to meet the English army marching south from Calais, the ponderous, exuberant, leg-weary king was planning to besiege Boulogne. It had long been in his mind to do this, and without caring for the success of the joint campaign he had worked out with Charles, he determined on this costly indulgence. In September he wrote to his wife of the busy time he was having: 'we be so occupied, and have so much to do in foreseeing and caring for everything ourself'. He told her eagerly how he had achieved 'somewhat of importance' by taking the outworks of the castle, and how progress was being delayed because 'our provision of powder is not come out of Flanders as we thought it would'. When his health allowed it, he spent long, tiring days in the field: he was a grown boy playing soldiers on a grand scale. Haughtily he refused to listen to French overtures for peace. He told Francis he could do nothing without consulting his ally, but Henry was probably more concerned about not being cheated at the last minute from taking Boulogne. He hardly listened when Charles sent the bishop of Arras to urge him to give up the siege and advance on Paris. Boulogne surrendered on 14 September, and at the head of his troops, Henry entered the town in triumph. He was satisfied. The French checked his attempt to take Montreuil further along the coast, but he, physically and emotionally exhausted, was anxious to return to England and negotiate for peace. But, he insisted, Boulogne must remain in English hands.

Although his siege of Boulogne had destroyed their plan for a joint invasion of the heart-land of France, Henry had punctiliously informed Charles of all French peace-feelers, and had assured him that he would never make a separate peace 'although he [Francis] would for our particular satisfaction make us never so large a proffer'. But Charles did not respond in the same way. He made a peace of his own at Crespy on 19 September, once Francis had promised that he would oppose and no longer help the Turks and the Lutherans. Henry gave the treaty a hasty, heavily qualified acquiescence, but he could not disguise the fact that he had been left to continue the war on his own. Francis offered to discuss terms and Charles to mediate, but Henry would not budge on the destiny of Boulogne. To his ambassador at the Imperial court he admitted that Francis had offered to pay the arrears of his 1525 pension, and to order the Scots to come to terms; '. . . if they shall also renounce all the claim they can make to Boulogne and Boullougnois (which we have now in our possession), and also surrender unto us the whole County of Guisnez, we will be contented to condescend to an agreement'. Francis, however, could not swallow this indignity. His son's soldiers kept up a steady pressure against Norfolk's garrison in the town, and later they attacked Guînes. Henry appealed to Charles for military aid. Charles refused, and at Brussels in November tried to mollify Gardiner and Hertford, Henry's representatives, by explaining that, since approaching winter would forbid campaigning, he could probably do Henry better service by restraining Francis as his partner than by opposing him on the battlefield. However true this might be, it did not bring Henry either men or money. Gardiner blamed the bishop of Arras, and wrote to him accusingly.

> His Highness, you were directed to say, was not averse to peace, but with conditions.... In view of a treaty which stipulates that the satisfaction of the King's Majesty shall be a preliminary of any peace ... can you pretend that it is with his Majesty's consent that he finds himself on his own? ... The King is spending only treasure, which is reparable. The Emperor is losing honour and credit, which is not reparable.

It was a splendid bit of debating, but it still left Henry dangerously isolated. Paris, Edinburgh, Vienna, Madrid, and Rome were all in accord. The international outlook as seen from London had rarely been so black.

The year 1545 gave Henry his fill of fighting. The rigours of winter did not daunt the French, and in the bleak days of January and February they tried to regain control of Boulogne harbour. Fortunately, or perhaps unfortunately, for Henry, Hertford's capable command of the garrison kept open communications between Boulogne and the English coast, but at the end of February, a Scottish victory near Jedburgh indicated what a difficult year 1545 was likely to be. Henry was continuing to sell crown lands and turning plate into coin, and yet expenses were still outstriding income. He was compelled to demand another benevolence from his nobles and merchants, and damage London's commercial prospects again by further debasement of the coinage. All this time he was impatiently struggling against pain and feverish, physical weakness. His leg needed rest, but he was far too busy seeing to things to give it any chance to improve: his general health required that he should relax and be abstemious, but Dr. Butts could not persuade him to follow any helpful routine of diet, rest, and exercise. In his attempts to kill his pain and quieten his nervous anxieties, he still ate and drank immoderately.

The climax of 1545 came in July and August. At Easter Henry offered to discuss terms with the Scots, but they, confident of French help, refused. By May they were recruiting troops for a major invasion of England, but Henry had no choice but to leave the northern frontier to the care of his wardens, because he had to be ready to repulse an expected French invasion from across the Channel. He had given the command of his defence forces to John Dudley, Lord Lisle, but he himself, enthusiastic as ever for naval affairs, jogged painfully if excitedly along the south coast inspecting repaired fortifications, reviewing troops, and mustering ships. Altogether that summer Henry could not have had less than 150,000 men under arms on the Scottish border, along the Channel coast, at strategic points on the west and east coasts, and on board ship. His fleet boasted about a hundred vessels, varying in size from the flagship, *Henry Grâce à Dieu*, to little ships of a few tons displacement; 16,000 sailors manned and armed them.

The French invasion fleet, 200 ships strong, sailed menacingly into the Solent on 18 July. Already it had made an unsuccessful attempt to land soldiers at Brighton; now it threatened the Isle of Wight. But during the next few days, Lisle used his ships in defence cleverly enough to force the French to withdraw. A second French attempt in mid-August had no better success, and this time Lisle chased the enemy across the Channel and raided several Norman ports in revenge. Henry was jubilant to think that his ships had beaten back the French, and now commanded the Channel. His precious Boulogne had held out during the difficult weeks, thanks partly to an outbreak of plague among the French siege troops, and the Scottish invasion had been decisively repulsed. He could not help feeling strong and boastful. Charles and Francis were both showing new respect: Charles offered money and arbitration, Francis talked about making peace. Henry's natural elation and self-satisfaction temporarily improved his health. He went hawking again.

The Scots had to endure the consequences of this mixture of relief and aggressiveness. Hertford crossed the border in September, and ferociously destroyed, burnt, or damaged everything his troops could lay hands on from castles and monasteries to mill-wheels and standing crops. The southern Scots endured a miserable winter. More and more of them murmured against the government and especially against Cardinal Beaton. The earl of Cassilis, spying a chance of overthrowing the pro-French faction, sought Henry's co-operation and asked for his sanction for the assassination of Beaton. Henry could not countenance such a dastardly act officially, but through his ministers he left Cassilis in no doubt that the service would be acceptable to him. In March 1546 Beaton made himself more unpopular in Scotland by sending a religious reformer to the stake, and two months later assassins murdered him in St. Andrews. Henry rewarded the murderers, and later succeeded in rescuing some of them from the avenging hands of Beaton's friends.

During that winter, however, Henry had comparatively little time to give to Scottish affairs. The French war was still dragging on with occasional clashes in the Channel and desultory fighting round Boulogne, but the main activity was diplomatic. Through Paget Henry was flirting again with a Lutheran alliance, and the Lutheran princes added their voice to the increasing chorus of ministers who urged him to make peace. But Henry showed no haste at all. Norfolk and others constantly reminded him of his desperate financial straits: Gardiner deplored the effect of the long war on commerce, and Wriothesley confessed that he was at his wits' end 'how we shall possibly make shift for the next three months'. But Henry's mind was fixed on using his apparent friendship with the Lutherans to frighten Charles into renewing his old alliance and guaranteeing England's possession of Boulogne. Councillors grew restless and bravely critical: they did not think Boulogne worth the expense and the risk. But Henry went his own way, and in March 1546 achieved his end. Charles became his ally again. Only now was Henry prepared to treat with Francis, not drawn by 'froward dealing', but 'contented to give ear to friendly and honourable conditions'. He declared that he was ready to negotiate about the arrears of pension due to him, and to discuss selling back to France land which he held round Boulogne and Guînes, but he insisted that he should continue to hold 'as a fisher town' Boulogne itself, 'which we have royally conquered in our just wars'. Negotiations dragged wearily on. At one point Henry made threatening preparations to reopen the campaign, but in June Francis gave way. For what it was worth, Henry's case, modified in the last stages of the negotiations by his ambassador, Paget, triumphed. The peace of Ardres decided that England should hold Boulogne and district until 1554, and in that year the French crown should redeem it for two million crowns. In the

meantime Francis was to pay Henry his pension, and help him force
the Scots to return to the terms of the Treaty of Greenwich. The
prospect of Prince Edward marrying Queen Mary came alive again.

The Father of his people

During these years of war and diplomacy, the struggle between the
theological reformers and traditionalists had continued unabated. In the
council chamber Cranmer successfully defended such innovations as
the English Bible and the destruction of shrines and relics, and in his
study quietly continued drafting new forms of services which years
later he was able to embody in the English prayer book. Gardiner,
Tunstal, and Norfolk worked in their different ways to reverse the
growing movement towards reform, and to keep the doctrine and
liturgy of the church as near to the Roman pattern as possible. In 1543
they congratulated themselves on a notable victory when Henry issued
A Necessary Doctrine and Erudition for any Christian Man, for this new
official statement of belief, commonly called *The King's Book*, held fast
to such orthodoxies as transubstantiation and the celibacy of the clergy.
In his preface to this 'true and perfect doctrine for all his people',
Henry again warned his subjects against reading the Scriptures too
enthusiastically and without the guidance of orthodox interpretation.
Chapuys summed it up when he reported to Charles V that *The King's
Book* restored 'ceremonies and other things of the Christian religion to
their first state, except what concerns the authority of the Apostolic See'.

Rooting out heresy concerned the lords during the session of parliament which opened in the autumn of 1545, but their debates only
emphasised the differences that existed among them. Eventually they
sent a much-amended bill down to the commons, only to see it rejected
by the lower house. Nothing tangible resulted from many hours of
debating. At the close of the session, appropriately on Christmas Eve,
Henry addressed both houses. In a fatherly manner, his confidence and
assumption no less than ever, he appealed to members to show good
will towards each other on theological matters. He began what was
destined to be his last public address by explaining that, good though
his lord chancellor might be, he could not 'open and set forth my mind
and meaning, and the secrets of my heart' as well as he could himself.
Through 'master Speaker' he wished to thank the commons for their

expression of loyalty, for the subsidy which would defray 'our great charges which we have lately sustained, as well in defence of our and your enemies', and for committing the chantries 'to mine order and disposition'. He rejoiced that such excellent relations existed between crown and people: '. . . no prince in the world more favoureth his subjects than I do you, nor no subjects or commons more love and obey their sovereign lord than I perceive you do me . . .'. But he deplored the lack of charity which his subjects showed to one another. They all knew how St. Paul had praised that most excellent gift of charity; 'behold then, what love and charity is amongst you, when the one calleth the other heretic and Anabaptist, and he calleth him again Papist, hypocrite, and Pharisee?' The chief blame Henry placed on the shoulders of the clergy who all preached different interpretations of the Scriptures. 'Alas how can the poor souls live in concord when you preachers sow amongst them in your sermons debate and discord: of you they look for light, and you bring them darkness.' But laymen were not blameless. They persisted in misusing their privilege of reading the Bible in English. The Scriptures were not a matter for argument, and Henry deplored hearing 'how unreverently that most precious jewel the word of God is disputed, rhymed, sung, and jangled in every alehouse and tavern'. It was a remarkable swan song, not least because he who had shown such a mixture of kindness and cruelty, patience and intolerance in his own life should choose to extol the virtues of charity to his people.

Materialism, zeal, and intolerance ousted charity from sixteenth-century life, and neither the law nor a royal sermon could diminish the theological struggle. Throughout 1546 it continued as fiercely as ever. Fortune swung first one way and then another. During the first half of the year, when Henry desperately needed the support of Emperor Charles, the traditionalists seemed to be gaining some lost ground. Gardiner, hunting for heretics and heretical writings, found useful colleagues in the solicitor-general, Sir Richard Rich, and in Wriothesley, newly appointed lord chancellor in place of Audley, who had died in 1544. They had Shaxton and Latimer charged and imprisoned. Anne Askew, another prisoner, they hoped would give them information which would implicate others, including, probably, the queen herself, and after the rack had wrung nothing out of Anne, they burnt her alive at Smithfield. Even Cranmer stood in imminent danger of arrest. But counter-influences were also at work. For no clear reason Henry appointed as Edward's tutors four men, Cox, Cheke, Cooke, and Ascham, who, if not extreme reformers, were decidedly not opposed to reform. Hertford, uncle of the prince, returned to court, and he and Lisle, heroes both fresh from the wars, sided with Cranmer. That autumn Henry and Cranmer were discussing ways and means of turning the mass into a communion service, and in November Gardiner, after refusing to humour Henry in a land deal, found himself out of favour, no longer summoned to council meetings. Worse still for the traditionalists, Surrey, the heir of Norfolk, foolishly roused in Henry the old, implacable hostility against possible pretenders to the throne, which in previous years had sealed the fate of Edmund de la Pole, Buckingham, and probably even the old countess of Salisbury. Wishing to draw attention to his claim to be descended from Edward the Confessor, Surrey had amended his coat-of-arms so that the royal arms were given pride of place in the first quarter. This alone alarmed Henry, but Surrey made his presumption worse first by cynically advising his sister to do her bit towards increasing the family's influence by becoming Henry's mistress, and secondly by openly advocating that when Henry died Norfolk should be appointed regent. Henry might have been very ill, but no one could throw down such a challenge to the prerogative with impunity. Surrey and Norfolk were both arrested on 12 December 1546. Six weeks later Surrey perished on Tower Hill, and but for Henry's own death occurring just in time, Norfolk too would have been executed at the end of January 1547.

Henry's mind and will remained remarkably active to the last day he lived. Throughout 1546 his body became increasingly burdensome. The ulcers on his legs spread, and the pain and feverish condition which they induced sapped his strength. Doctors tried the painful treatment of cauterising the ulcers, but this did not cure them. Henry forced himself to carry out his duties attending council meetings, and receiving envoys and ambassadors. At times he had to surrender to pain and weakness and stay in bed, but in his last year of life he drove himself hard and with great courage. The suspected treachery of Surrey and Norfolk goaded him to extraordinary, physical activity, but relapse inevitably followed. He died at Whitehall in the early hours of 28 January 1547. Cranmer, who was with him at the end, later assured ministers and courtiers that their king had died in the faith of Christ.

In his last few weeks, Henry did what he could to ensure a happy future for his wife and his son. He gave orders that Queen Catherine should always be treated and honoured in the way she would have been had he continued to live. He bade Princess Mary try and be a mother to Prince Edward, and he nominated a regency council in which he hoped he had achieved a nice balance between those who sought to advance and those who wished to retard change. Cranmer, Hertford, Tunstal, Wriothesley and the rest were all trusted servants, who in their different ways had served the crown well. They knew precisely what Henry required to be done, for at the end of December he set it down clearly in his will. His son, Edward, and the heirs of his body lawfully begotten were to inherit 'the imperial crown and realm of England and Ireland, our title to France, with all dignities, honours, pre-eminences, prerogatives, authorities, jurisdictions, lands, and posses-sions'. If that line failed, then Mary and her heirs should succeed, and then, if necessary, Elizabeth and her heirs. Should these alternatives not make enough provision—a most unlikely event—Henry willed that the crown should pass to the descendants of his sister Mary. He overlooked Mary Stuart, his sister Margaret's grandchild. But even kings as absolute as Henry Tudor have imperfect control from the grave. They, like the rest of us, can only express their wishes, appoint their executors, and leave the rest in the hands of God and future generations.

Index

Names of places are printed in italics
The numerals in **bold** type refer to the figure-numbers of the illustrations

Adrian VI (pope, 1522–3), 50, 53
Aigues-Mortes, Languedoc, 125
Angus, sixth earl of, 32, 64, 143
Arthur, prince of Wales (d. 1502), 15–16, 37, 58, 63, 68, 93
Aske, Robert (exec. 1537), 120–1, 123
Audley, Sir Thomas (speaker and lord chancellor), 99, 113, 136, 149

Balinghem, near Calais, 44, 46
Barnes, Dr. Robert (exec. 1541), 73, 131, 135
Barton, Elizabeth (exec. 1534), 99–100, 102–3
Beaton, David (cardinal, d. 1546), 138, 140, 142–3, 146–7
Bell, Dr. John, 62, 69
Bellay, Jean du (bishop of Paris), 77, 98, 101, 103
Blount, Elizabeth, 35, 56, 60
Boleyn, Anne (exec. 1536), 57, 66, 75, 95, 96, 98, 99–100, 102–3, 105, 116, 118, **9**; early life, 59–61; negotiations concerning, 63–65, 67, 72–74, 76–79, 83–89; attitude to Wolsey, 71–72; supporters and family at court, 59–60, 74, 84, 101; honours, 76, 88; marriage, 90–92; coronation, 92–94; birth of Elizabeth, 96; downfall, 108, 110, 112–15, 137
Boleyn, Lady Elizabeth, 59
Boleyn, George, Viscount Rochford, 95, 114–15
Boleyn, Mary, Mistress Carey, 59, 63, 112
Boleyn, Thomas, earl of Wiltshire, 59, 66, 74, 76–77, 87, 92, 113, 115
Boulogne, 89, 143–7
Brandon, Charles—*see* Suffolk
Buckingham, Edward, third duke of (exec. 1521), 46–47, 150
Butts, Dr. William, 66, 108, 145

Calais, 25, 28–29, 40, 44–46, 49, 52, 88–89, 115, 124–5, 143
Cambrai, league of (1508), 19, 23; treaty of, 71
Campeggio, Lorenzo (cardinal), 40, 50, 65–72
Carew, Nicholas, 35, 43, 84
Carey, William, 59, 66
Cassilis, earl of, 139, 143, 146–7
Castello, Hadrian de (cardinal), 40

Catherine of Aragon (d. 1536), 21–25, 27, 30, 35, 37, 40–41, 44, 46–47, 50, 53, 59, 60–61, 63–66, 69, 71, 73–77, 79, 85, 87–88, 94, 96, 98, 103, 108, 112–13, 134, **8**; marriage, 16–20; birth of Mary, 34; growing unhappiness, 56–58; conflict with Henry, 62–63, 67–68, 70, 84, 91–93, 100, 107; appeals to Rome, 83–84, 110–11; death, 111
Chapuys, Eustace (Imperial ambassador), 78, 84, 88, 90, 92, 96–97, 100, 107–8, 110–13, 116, 137, 141, 148
Charles V (emperor, 1519–58), 32, 52–54, 58, 67–68, 75, 88, 90–92, 95, 107, 109–10, 112–13, 118, 123–5, 128, 133–8, 141–9, **2**; betrothal to Mary, Henry's sister, 18–19, 26, 30; treaty of Noyon, 33, 39; elected emperor, 40–45; betrothal to Henry's daughter, 46, 49–51; league of Cognac, 55–56; sack of Rome, 62; treaty of Barcelona, 70; treaty of Cambrai, 71; reactions to Henry's marriage problem, 62–63, 69, 76–77, 79, 87, 94, 96–97; peace of Crespy, 144
Clement VII (pope, 1523–34), 48, 69, 70, 78–79, 84, 86, 89–90, 107; election, 53; league of Cognac, 55; imprisonment; 62, 65; crowns Charles V, 76; attitude to Henry's marriage, 63–67, 70–72, 76, 77, 83, 87, 94–98, 101, 103; death, 108
Clerk, John (bishop), 48, 70, 72
Cleves, Anne of, 128, 130–1, 133–4, 141, **11**
Cognac, league of (1526), 55, 58, 62
Cranmer, Thomas (archbishop of Canterbury, 1533–56), 73, 99, 119, 123, 133, 140, 150–1, **23**; created archbishop, 89–90; duties concerned with Queen Anne, 91–96; trial of Anne, 114–15; as a reformer, 129–30, 135–6, 148–9
Cromwell, Thomas (exec. 1540), 87–89, 94, 97, 100, 104–5, 107, 109, 116, 118–22, 125–6, 129–31, 134–5, 139, 142, **22**; rise to power, 79–80; church policy, 85, 91, 98–99, 117; foreign policy, 113–14, 128; death, 133
Culpeper, Thomas (exec. 1541), 136–7

Dacres, Thomas, Lord, 53, 136
Darcy, Thomas, Lord, 85, 119–21
Dereham, Francis (exec. 1541), 136–7
Dorset, Thomas, second marquis, 24, 28–29, 32, 47

Douglas, Lady Mary (Henry's niece), 64, 118, 143
Dudley, John, Viscount Lisle, 146, 150
Dunstable, 92, 94–95

Edward IV (king, 1461–83), 15, 79, 123
Edward, prince of Wales (afterwards Edward VI), 122–4, 136, 139–40, 148, 150–1, **21, 24, 28**
Eleanor, sister of Charles V, 18–19, 88
Elizabeth, princess (afterwards Elizabeth I), 60, 94, 96, 101, 109, 118, 123–4, 151, **20**
Elizabeth of York (queen, 1486–1503), 15
Erasmus, Desiderius, 13–14, 22, 37, 48, 65

Ferdinand of Aragon (d. 1516), 16, 19–20, 23–25, 27, 29, 32–33, 67
Fisher, John (bishop of Rochester, exec. 1535), 62, 70, 75–76, 99, 105, 109–10, **17**
Fitzroy, Henry (duke of Richmond, d. 1536), 36, 46–47, 56, 58, 118
Fitzwilliam, William (earl of Southampton), 74, 77, 121
Flodden (battle of, 1513), 26, 53, 134, 138
Fox, Richard (bishop, d. 1528), 18, 19, 21, 23, 28
Foxe, Edward, 65, 73, 87
Francis I (king, 1515–47), 19, 30, 44, 49–50, 58–59, 63, 67, 71, 75, 85, 90, 110, 123, 125, 128, 131, 133, 137, 141, 148, **3**; accession, 31; early diplomacy, 32–33; imperial ambitions, 39–43; captive, 53–55; attitude to Anne, 73, 77, 83, 87–89, 94–95, 97–98, 103; claims on Milan, 111, 118–19; marriage treaty proposals, 101, 108–9, 124; relations with Scotland, 32, 124, 135–6, 138, 142–4, 146–7
Fuenterrabia, western Pyrenees, 24, 28, 32, 37

Gardiner, Stephen (bishop), 65, 69, 73, 79, 84, 88, 94, 95, 97–98, 131, 133–5, 140, 145, 147–8, 150
Glencairn, earl of, 139, 143
Grace, pilgrimage of, 120–2
Grammont, Gabriel de (cardinal), 58, 77, 87, 90
Greenwich, convent of, 88; palace of, 19–20, 30, 34, 37, 39, 44, 50, 65, 71, 84–85, 87, 90, 93–94, 96, 111–14, 131, **4**; treaty of (1543), 140, 142, 148
Grey, Lord Leonard, 135–6
Guînes, near *Calais*, 43–44, 144–5, 147

Hall, Edward (historian, d. 1547), 13, 22, 35, 37, 68–69, 85, 119, 131–2
Hampton Court, 50, 115, 123, 136, 140
Henry VII (king, 1485–1509), 14–19, 21, 23, 47, 49, 67, 143
Henry VIII (king, 1509–47), ancestry, 14–16; coronation, 13, 19; first marriage,

16–20; foreign policy, 23–27, 50–55, 58–59, 88–89, 95–96, 113, 123–5, 128, 141–8; Elizabeth Blount, 35–36; naval matters, 36–37; dissatisfaction with his first marriage, 57–58, 60–71, 73–74, 79; relations with Anne Boleyn, 59–61, 88, 90–91, 108, 110, 112–13; struggle against papacy, 77–78, 81–82, 85–91, 95, 97; defiance of Catherine and Mary, 100, 107–111; act of succession, 101–8; Jane Seymour, 110, 115, 122–3; Anne of Cleves, 128, 130–1, 133; Catherine Howard, 131–7; theology, 48, 128–30, 135, 148–50; Scotland, 135, 138–40, 142–3, 146–7; Ireland, 135; Catherine Parr, 140–1; death, 150; **1, 14, 15, 18, 24, 25, 26, 27, 28**
Howard, Catherine (exec. 1542), 131, 133–4, 136–7, **12**

Isabella of Castile (queen, 1474–1504), 16–17, 108

James IV of Scotland (king, 1488–1513), 15, 26, 138
James V of Scotland (king, 1513–42), 124–5, 135–6, 138–9
Joanna of Castile, 18–19
Julius II (pope, 1503–13), 17, 23, 64, 67, 69

Knight, Dr. William, 63–65

Latimer, Hugh (bishop, exec. 1555), 109, 130, 149
Lautrec, Sieur de (French general), 63, 66–67
Leo X (pope, 1513–21), 27, 29, 32, 40–41, 48–50
Lille (treaty of, 1513), 26–27
London, Blackfriars, 69–70, 75; *Charterhouse*, 104, 165; *Guildhall*, 137; *Marshalsea prison*, 104; *Newgate prison*, 105; *St. Paul's*, 41, 53; *Smithfield*, 135, 149; *Tower of*, 114, 121, 131, 133, 135–7; *Tyburn*, 103–4, 133, 137
Louis XII (king, 1498–1515), 18, 25–27, 29–30, 67
Luther, Martin (1483–1546), 46, 48, 65, 73, 83

Margaret Tudor (queen of Scotland, d. 1541), 15, 27, 32, 35, 64, 136, 138, 151
Marguerite de Valois (sister of Francis I), 19, 88
Marignano (battle of, 1515), 32, 34
Marillac, Charles de (French ambassador), 134–5, 141
Mary Tudor, duchess of Suffolk, 15, 18, 26–27, 30–31, 41–42, 76

Mary Tudor (afterwards Queen Mary I), 34, 40–41, 45–47, 50–51, 54–58, 68, 76, 84, 96, 100–1, 107–11, 115–16, 118, 123–4, 151, **19**

Maximilian I (emperor, 1493–1519), 18, 23–27, 29, 32–34, 39, 40–42

Mendoza, Don Inigo de (Imperial ambassador), 58, 62, 69

Monasteries, suppression of, 116–17, 122

More, Sir Thomas (lord chancellor, exec. 1535), 37, 48, 52, 61, 74–75, 79, 86, 99, 102–3, 105, 110, **16**

Nice (treaty of, 1538), 124, 138

Norfolk, Thomas, second duke of, and earl of Surrey (d. 1524), 23–26, 38–39, 47

Norfolk, Thomas, third duke of, and earl of Surrey (d. 1554), 39, 51, 71–72, 74, 76–77, 79, 81, 84–85, 88, 91, 95, 98, 113–14, 118, 120–3, 131, 134, 136, 139, 143, 145, 147–8, 150

Noyon (treaty of, 1516), 33, 39

Observant friars, 96, 99–100, 104

Pace, Richard (ambassador), 33, 41–42, 48, 50

Paget, Sir William, 147

Parr, Catherine (married Henry 1543), 140–1, 151, **13**

Paul III (pope, 1534–49), 108–110, 119, 123–7, 135, 141

Peto, William (friar), 87–88

Pole, Edmund de la, earl of Suffolk, 25, 47, 53, 150

Pole, Sir Geoffrey, 125

Pole, Reginald (cardinal), 100, 123, 125–6

Pole, Richard de la, 53

Pommeraye, Giles de la, 85, 87, 90

Puebla, Roderijo de (Spanish ambassador), 17, 69

Pyle (abbot of Furness), 122

Reynolds, Richard (exec. 1535), 104–5

Richmond, 20, 22, 31, 37, 50, 64, 116, 133, **5**

Rochford, Lady Jane (exec. 1542), 136–7

Rochford, Viscount—see Boleyn, George

Ruthal, Thomas (bishop), 21, 28, 38

St. Leger, Sir Anthony, 135, 139

Salisbury, Mary, countess of (exec. 1541), 99, 125, 136, 150

Sampson, Dr. Richard (bishop), 69, 133

Seymour, Edward, earl of Hertford, 115, 136, 143, 145–6, 150–1

Seymour, Jane (d. 1533), 110, 112–13, 115–16, 118, 122–3, 134, 140, **10**

Seymour, Sir John, 110

Seymour, Sir Thomas (admiral), 140

Sforza, Christina, 124, 126

Sforza, Francesco, duke of Milan (d. 1535), 111, 124

Sforza, Massimiliano, duke of Milan (d. 1530), 32

Shaxton, Nicholas (bishop), 109, 149

Shrewsbury, George, fourth earl of, 25, 59

Skelton, John (poet), 28, 34, 55

Smeaton, Mark (exec. 1536), 113–14

Solway Moss (battle of, 1542), 139

Stewart, Henry, Lord Methuen, 64

Stewart, John, duke of Albany, 32, 40

Stokesley, John (bishop), 74, 82, 91, 94, 96

Stuart, Mary queen of Scots, 100, 139–40, 148, 151

Suffolk, earl of—see Pole

Suffolk, Charles Brandon, duke of, 29–32, 35, 42, 47, 52, 62, 70–72, 74, 76, 79, 84, 100, 113, 123, 143

Surrey, earl of—see Norfolk

Syon abbey, 104–5, 137

Thérouanne (siege of, 1513), 25–26, 32

Tournai, 26–27, 29, 32, 40, 42

Trinity House, corporation of, 36–37

Tuke, Sir Brian, 82–83

Tunstal, Cuthbert (bishop), 32, 41, 51, 53–55, 74, 82, 148, 151

Wallop, Sir John, 135, 142

Warham, William (archbishop), 19, 21, 23, 28–29, 33, 61, 70, 81, 83, 85, 88–89, 99, **7**

Westminster Abbey, 13, 15, 19, 81, 94

Westminster Palace, 20, 22, 81, 114

Whitehall (York House), 41, 73, 90, 93, 114–15

Winchester, bishop of—see Fox and Gardiner

Windsor, 18, 37, 50–51, 84, 88, 128

Wolsey, Thomas, 27, 31–34, 36, 41–42, 44–45, 47–49, 55, 57–59, 61, 63, 74–75, 80, 82, 84, 107, **6**; rise to power, 28–30; controls government during plague, 38–39; appointed cardinal, 40; aspires to papacy, 50, 53; financial policy, 51–54; Henry's marriage affairs, 64–71; downfall, 72–73; arrest and death, 78–79

Wriothesley, Sir Thomas (secretary and chancellor), 126, 136, 147, 149, 151

Wyatt, Sir Thomas, 114, 124, 135

York, 29, 121–2, 136

York House—see Whitehall